"The authors describe this book—the fruit of a collaborative writing project among seasoned leaders—as a 'love letter to pastors,' and so it is! Readers enter into a lively conversation between wise clergy colleagues and mentors, examining the significance and challenges of ministry that at its best is both pastoral and political. In these realistic accounts of pastoral leadership grounded in the church's call to care for the precious and complicated world that God so loves, new and experienced pastors and lay leaders will encounter surprising resonances, bracing practical wisdom, and a rekindled commitment to community well-being."

—CYNTHIA G. LINDNER,
Director of Ministry Studies, The Divinity School, The University of Chicago

"The truth that pastors need peers is often spoken and difficult to realize. This book is an inspiring how-to guide where seven practitioner-authors tell how they have formed pastor peer groups based on a common purpose—being 'political pastors' working for the good of their neighbors. Biblical reflection, practical tools, and stories are mixed in a way that provide something inspiring and challenging for anyone who cares for congregations and those who lead them."

—DAVID L. ODOM,
Executive Director, Leadership Education, Duke Divinity

"*Seek the Well-Being of the City* is an excellent resource. I've never read anything just like it. Seven ecumenical pastors provide collaborative guidance for community building and pastoral care. Including practical and deeply insightful wisdom, the authors address dilemmas and shared congregational challenges. They draw from one another lessons of the past and offer to each other evidence-informed solutions. The authors synthesize their work into a tapestry of guidance, insight, and practice wisdom. Enjoy!"

—HELEN HARRIS,
Associate Professor Emeritus of Social Work, Baylor University

"Designed for clergy seeking to make a tangible difference, *Seek the Well-Being of the City* offers practical strategies for contextual analysis, ongoing learning, and helping leaders develop tactics for understanding their communities deeply. Through real-world examples and testimonial insights, ministers are encouraged to identify challenges, engage stakeholders, and implement faith-driven solutions for lasting transformation. Whether revitalizing congregations or addressing social issues, this book empowers clergy to navigate complexity with clarity, ensuring their ministry fosters meaningful, sustainable impact in their communities."

—MYCAL BRICKHOUSE,
Director of Program and Grants, Leadership Education,
Duke Divinity School

Seek the Well-Being of the City

Seek the Well-Being of the City

Pastoral Leadership in Community

Derek R. Nelson, Erica Knisely,
Jason R. McConnell, Natalie Aho,
Leslie King, Amy Howard,
and Wes Spears-Newsome

CASCADE *Books* • Eugene, Oregon

SEEK THE WELL-BEING OF THE CITY
Pastoral Leadership in Community

Copyright © 2025 Wipf and Stock. All rights reserved. Except for brief quotations in critical publications or reviews, no part of this book may be reproduced in any manner without prior written permission from the publisher. Write: Permissions, Wipf and Stock Publishers, 199 W. 8th Ave., Suite 3, Eugene, OR 97401.

Cascade Books
An Imprint of Wipf and Stock Publishers
199 W. 8th Ave., Suite 3
Eugene, OR 97401

www.wipfandstock.com

PAPERBACK ISBN: 979-8-3852-1549-2
HARDCOVER ISBN: 979-8-3852-1550-8
EBOOK ISBN: 979-8-3852-1551-5

Cataloguing-in-Publication data:

Names: Nelson, Derek R., author. | Knisely, Erica, author. | McConnell, Jason R., author. | Aho, Natalie, author. | King, Leslie, author. | Howard, Amy, author. | Spears-Newsome, Wesley, author.

Title: Seek the well-being of the city : pastoral leadership in community / Derek R. Nelson, Erica Knisely, Jason R. McConnell, Natalie Aho, Leslie King, Amy Howard, and Wesley Spears-Newsome.

Description: Eugene, OR: Cascade Books, 2025 | Includes bibliographical references.

Identifiers: ISBN 979-8-3852-1549-2 (paperback) | ISBN 979-8-3852-1550-8 (hardcover) | ISBN 979-8-3852-1551-5 (ebook)

Subjects: LCSH: Communities—Religious aspects—Christianity. | Community organization. | Parishes.

Classification: BV625 S44 2025 (paperback) | BV625 (ebook)

07/11/25

Unless otherwise noted, the Scripture quotations contained herein are from the New Revised Standard Version, 1989 by the Division of Christian Education of the National Council of the Churches of Christ in the U.S.A. Used by permission. All rights reserved.

This book is dedicated to parish pastors.
You find ways to love communities,
which is one of the very few things truly worth doing.

Contents

Introduction   1

PART I. KNOWING IN COMMUNITY

1. Clergy Learning Communities   15
2. Growing Leadership Capacities   26
3. Pastor as Political Leader   34

PART II. LEADING IN COMMUNITY

4. Learning the Layers of Your Community   49
5. Discerning Where and How to Act   68
6. Responding with Your Community   80
7. Reflecting on Your Power   99

PART III. PERSISTING IN COMMUNITY

8. Expecting and Managing Resistance   113
9. The Joy of Ministry in Community   122

Bibliography   127

Introduction

THIS BOOK IS A love letter to pastors, however you define that word. It has been written by a group of people who have gathered, watched, encouraged, learned from, and celebrated with pastors over many years. All of us are pastors or are married to pastors who serve in local congregations.

We are here because, in 2008, the Lilly Endowment, Inc. launched the Early Career Leadership Development Initiative and funded programs at fifteen institutions throughout the United States. Collectively, as leaders and participants in these programs, we have engaged with hundreds of ministers serving congregations across the United States from every type of community and denominational body in the Christian faith. Our participating clergy represented a diversity of gender, race, social class, age, ability, and sexual orientation. Because of the unique roots of this book as a quite specific collaborative initiative, and especially because of the truly unusual circumstances of this book's writing, we want to introduce ourselves right at the beginning, even though you might not be sure yet whether you particularly care about us or about our initiative.

WHO WE ARE

Derek Nelson is a Lutheran (ELCA) pastor who serves as a professor of religion at Wabash College in Crawfordsville, Indiana. He directed the Wabash Pastoral Leadership Program at Wabash College from 2012 to 2021. That program was the first in the

Early Career Pastoral Leadership Development Initiative funded by Lilly Endowment, Inc. A total of seventeen leadership programs for pastors was created and funded by that initiative. Since 2013, he has been the director of the Early Career coordination work of those seventeen programs, also based at Wabash College. He has served as a parish pastor, dean of a local ministerium, and with his national church body on a number of justice-related initiatives. He writes a lot, but this is the most fun he's had writing a book.

Natalie Aho served as the director of development for the Association of Welcoming and Affirming Baptists. She has spent over two and a half decades as a professional in communications, program development, fundraising, and as an educator. She was previously employed at Wake Forest University School of Divinity as the program manager for the Baptist Commons and as program director for three Lilly Endowment grants, including their Early Career Leadership Development Initiative called Clergy in Community. She is married to Rev. Dr. Chris Aho, who has been in pastoral work for more than twenty-four years. He is now the director of thriving congregations for the Cooperative Baptist Fellowship. They live in Durham, North Carolina, with their two fantastic sons and are proud members of Watts Street Baptist Church. She found writing this book with a group of colleagues who became friends to be way more fun than the grant writing she usually does.

Leslie King has been a Presbyterian pastor since 1994, serving in Osawatomie, Kansas, and Waco, Texas. She completed her DMin in 2010. She sits on the board of the Cobb Institute and has a deep interest in Alfred North Whitehead and his impact on the Reformed tradition. She is wife to DJ and they enjoy Cody, Katie, and Claire, their young adult children. Their family is a host of animals. Leslie has a love of organizational development, amassed five hundred hours toward yoga competency, and enjoys her running . . . though others perceive her to be walking.

Wes Spears-Newsome is a Baptist pastor who works as an associate focused on community work, communications and outreach, and youth ministry. Particular through-lines of his work are LGBTQ inclusion and affordable housing. He's also a writer

INTRODUCTION

of everything from science fiction/fantasy to theological reflection around issues of immigration and incarceration. Wes lives with his wife and young daughter, along with his mother-in-law, in Cary, North Carolina.

Amy Howard is a priest and healing prayer minister in the Anglican diocese of New England. She and her husband are both church planters and pastors, and Amy is the founder and director of Encounter Culture, a teaching, equipping, and retreat-based ministry formed to see people set free by the power of the Holy Spirit and released to walk in the fullness of their identity and mission as men and women created in the image of God. She joined a Lilly-funded cohort in 2020 and found a well-spring of inspiration, courage to engage the surrounding community in new and creative ways, and friendships with other like-minded clergy that continue to challenge and bless. Amy, her husband, their six boys, and a constantly varying number of smaller creatures currently reside on a family farm and orchard in New Hampshire.

Erica Knisely is a Presbyterian pastor who serves as minister of formation and outreach with St. Andrew's Presbyterian Church in Austin, Texas. She helped lead the lifelong learning department at Austin Seminary for eight years and, in that capacity, worked closely with early career pastors through the Pastoral Leadership for Public Life Program (2014–2023). She moved to Austin in 2001 to study at the LBJ School of Public Affairs at the University of Texas at Austin, and never left Central Texas. After earning her degree, she spent six years helping to expand the state's community healthcare infrastructure before entering another round of graduate studies. Erica has a nearly insatiable need to learn, most recently dabbling in flamenco dance and samba drumming. She is partner to Patrick, whom she met in an improv comedy class, and Mama to Magnus, who makes her heart sing. The three live in Pflugerville, Texas, with their cats, Moose and Monkey.

Jason McConnell has served as senior pastor of the Franklin United Church and East Franklin Union Church in Franklin, Vermont, since 2004. He also serves as an adjunct professor of practical ministry, mentor in the Doctor of Ministry program, and co-director of the Ockenga Fellows Program at Gordon-Conwell Theological Seminary in South Hamilton, Massachusetts. In addition to spending time with his wife, Jennifer, and their four children, he enjoys Vermont outdoor activities including hiking, biking, kayaking, fishing, skiing, and snowshoeing.

HOW THIS BOOK CAME ABOUT

In September 2023, this group of seven curious learners gathered at Wabash College. Following our fearless leader, Barbara Ruehling, we wrestled with what to put on these pages for five long days and nights. Or really, we wrestled with what to not put on these pages, for there was no shortage of reflections, stories, and analysis that flowed from our experiences with the Early Career Leadership Development Initiative.

You did read that correctly; we wrote this book in five days through a process called a book sprint. A book sprint is a "highly collaborative process of knowledge production with a non-negotiable deadline. Over 5 days . . . authors are guided by a Book Sprints facilitator to develop a shared vision, outline the content, write in groups, and edit each other's work. The result is a book with a collective voice and shared authorship, rather than an edited volume written by individual authors."[1] We all agreed that the trust, humility, maturity, and imagination that was required of us during this week was a challenging experience. But it was also some of the most rewarding work we have ever done.

We use the word "we" a lot. All of us sit in, at, or near the congregational ministry, either now or in the immediate past. Not all of us are ordained ministers, but we all work with, as, or for pastors. We have tried to normally reserve the "we" for the seven of us who wrote the book. However, because all of us have been part of a number of clergy learning communities, or cohorts in various leadership programs, we sometimes draw on our experiences of those programs as leaders or participants. These experiences are

1. "Why Do a Book Sprint?"

INTRODUCTION

often shared as stories or illustrations, our own or those of our fellow clergy. We do primarily represent white, mainline Protestant congregations. However, we have tried to represent all ministers and communities through our examples and stories from within our cohorts. Because the well of experience is deep, it can be hard to know which "we" is in the bucket pulled up.

This book is primarily for clergy; however, we would be thrilled if our congregants were reading it too. The target career stage of our cohort programs was "early career," meaning those who are past their first five years of congregational work but are not yet in their second decade. We never limited this definition by age. Second- (or third- or fourth-) career pastors still follow the same ministerial career arc, even if they bring more life experience to the job. We also believe those who are exploring a call to ministry may benefit from reading our work. We hope this book confirms the joy and transformation you hope ministry will bring. And we pray it will prepare you for the challenges as well.

Our cohort experiences (whether one cycle or over ten years) were so profound, so transformative, so magical even, that we were eager to spill it onto these pages. When we brainstormed themes, we used words like *invitation, hospitality, dignity, care, confidence, leadership, imagination, capacity,* and *inspiration*. What a joy and gift it has been to journey alongside other ministers as we collectively experienced the transforming power of intentional engagement in layers of community. The joy can only be multiplied if we can bring you along with us. We hope that you see yourself in these pages, that you know you are not alone, that you find bread for the journey, that you build confidence in your engagement with civic and community leaders, and that you find new curiosity and imagination.

As with the nervous moments when you walk into the retreat room, unsure why you said yes to the invitation to join a clergy cohort, we were trepidatious about taking on this project. The stakes were even higher with this work; yes, we had to share trust, humility, and vulnerability. But now we were renouncing our private property, our most valued turn of phrase, our darlings. The gift, though, of reappropriating the now-collective good is worth the delight we have received. As a collective of authors who have edited and reedited each other's words, we have ceded ownership while having the courage to engage the writing with confidence and humility.

It takes some chutzpah to delete a paragraph somebody else wrote and then replace it with your own. It takes just as much courage to watch it happen to your own contribution! One of us compared the mutual writing and editing process to sending your kid to a babysitter and having them returned to you with a new haircut (and maybe a tattoo!).

We had some initial doubts as to whether or not the undertaking could even be possible. But it was truly remarkable to watch the different voices and perspectives fold into a unified text. Ultimately, we think it demonstrates that we practice what we preach. As you'll see in chapter 1, for an effective clergy learning community, we had a common purpose, ecumenical diversity, a shared covenant of collaboration, and a shared adventure. The endeavor was a microcosm of what we present in the following pages: leaders learning together to exit the safety of the four walls of their congregations to engage and bless one another. We turn now to a different time and place when pastors and seminarians gathered together to learn side by side in the context of a terrifying and uncertain political situation.

LIFE TOGETHER, AGAIN

Though we find ourselves quite distant from Germany in the 1930s, we believe there are some critical lessons in the story of Dietrich Bonhoeffer and his brief time with seminarians at a place called Finkenwalde. After receiving his PhD at a young age, Bonhoeffer ran into a big problem. German law prevented people from becoming professors before the age of twenty-five. To kill some time, he went to New York City to study at Union Theological Seminary; then he went to Barcelona, where he served as a pastor for awhile;

INTRODUCTION

then England; and for a while, he worked with the youth movement in Berlin.

He was very active in the church's struggle under the Nazi regime. Some Germans, who called themselves "German Christians," claimed it was their patriotic and even Christian duty to support their leader, the Fuehrer, with blind devotion. Bonhoeffer and millions of others disagreed. They formed a new organization called the Confessing Church. Its basic document, called the Barmen Declaration, said, in effect, that Jesus is Lord and Adolf Hitler is not.

The Confessing Church operated on a shoestring budget. It had a lot of people cheering it on from the outside, though, and Bonhoeffer was a prolific letter writer, asking for support and trying to tell the story of how the church's resistance to Hitler was going. The need for training pastors was clear, and so five seminaries were formed—one in 1935 in Finkenwalde, in modern-day Poland.

Finkenwalde was a grand experiment in education. Already in 1935, Bonhoeffer was thinking about what kind of leader would be needed in the postwar era. What kinds of skills and personal characteristics of integrity and strength of spirit would be needed as a leader in Germany after the war?

Things were going well until November 1937, when the Gestapo appeared without warning, arrested twenty-seven brothers, and sent them to prison. Before the seminary could conduct a graduation ceremony or even say goodbye, the whole place was abandoned. The students who had escaped arrest returned home to what felt like a prison anyway. They felt lost, confused, scared, and alone.

Bonhoeffer had been away from campus when the Gestapo arrived. To comfort the now scattered students, he wrote letters to every single one. But his primary focus was to write a book titled *Life Together*. This little book was his attempt to keep the spirit of the community at Finkenwalde alive. In it, he offers some wisdom about community, particularly the kind of community that helps pastors thrive, heal, and move forward.

First, Bonhoeffer insists that true community is a gift from God, not a human achievement. Even though we can create the conditions that facilitate it, such a community cannot be mandated or manufactured. The best community happens not in classrooms or formal meetings, but simply appears during unplanned sidebar conversations, around the dinner table, and over a pint at the pub.

Bonhoeffer helps us to see that we need each other, we are made for each other, and in receiving the other, we find ourselves. It's not an ideal to be realized by working really hard to make it more real. It's a reality already that might be graciously uncovered and revealed to us.

Second, Bonhoeffer helps us see how quickly we make an idol of community. The people who loved Finkenwalde missed it and were prone to romanticizing it. Bonhoeffer writes,

> Those who love their dream of a Christian community more than the Christian community itself become destroyers of that community, even though their personal intentions may be ever so honest, earnest and sacrificial ... This wishful dreaming ... makes the dreamer proud and pretentious ... The bright day of community dawns wherever the early morning mists of dreamy visions are lifting.[2]

Clergy often romanticize the deep community they experienced during a college ministry or their seminary days, but once they accept the call to ministry and land in a parish, they struggle to form meaningful friendships and find mutual support, intellectual stimulation, and vocational inspiration. Unfortunately, many clergy fall victim to their congregations' unrealistic expectations or the mundane tasks of ministry. They can't seem to find the right people to help them process their pain or expand their imagination.

It would be a mistake for most clergy to try to replicate Finkenwalde today. Times have changed and the context is different, but there is a reason why so many have been drawn to Bonhoeffer's vision in *Life Together* since it was originally published in 1939. We

---

2. Bonhoeffer, *Life Together*, 36–37.

crave the transformative power of true community! Is there a way to recapture his vision and contextualize it for today?

PASTORS TOGETHER, LEARNING ABOUT LIFE TOGETHER

In 2008, the Lilly Endowment launched the Early Career Leadership Development Initiative, based on the belief that transformative power is generated when clergy fully recognize and engage the multiple layers of community around them. The endowment funded fifteen institutions of higher education throughout the United States and helped them form a series of clergy learning cohorts to share life, develop their skills as leaders, build collaborative relationships with civic leaders, and increase pastoral capacity for engaging the community beyond their local churches.

The authors of this book have served as directors or participants in these cohorts, and we have all personally experienced the transformative power that emerges when clergy engage with the multiple layers of community around them. The need for this transformative power is even more profound in this age of a post-Christian, post-COVID-19, politically divided, secularized, and hyperlocal and yet also globally connected world. This book is our attempt to share the collective wisdom we've gained from these cohorts. They have shifted our thinking about ministry as something that primarily happens inside the church building to something that happens in and through the whole community.

The seventeenth-century Quaker George Fox insisted that no one refer to a building as a church. It must be called a "steeple house," even if it doesn't have a steeple. "Church" for Fox could only refer to people.[3] He thought the Church of England had gotten lazy and taken advantage of its favored role as the officially endorsed religious institution of the nation. He wanted to shake things up a bit by forcing people to recognize their responsibilities as Christians.

---

3. Placher and Nelson, *Readings in the History of Christian Theology*, 64.

A retired pastor said to an early career minister, "This is a *really* nice office! You aren't ever going to want to leave it . . . You better, though." Like George Fox, the retired pastor knew that real ministry moves outside the walls of the church building.

In the pages that follow, we hope to cast a vision for life together again. We want you to gain a clearer understanding of your vocation, reap the benefits of a learning community, and embrace your role as a political leader. In the end, we want you and your congregation to recognize the inescapable mutuality that connects us all. We invite you to join us on this journey as we continue to seek the transformative power of clergy engaging these multiple levels of community.

No one automatically knows how to do these things, so consider this book an invitation to something new. Not something you should have known or something you've been doing wrong, but something we hope will invigorate your ministry. Experiment and try new things. Don't be afraid to fail; we certainly have! Drawing not least from our mistakes, you may encounter more prescriptive language to save you a few headaches.

We have created a book that invites you into new postures of ministry, new methods of learning, and new strategies for engagement. We've divided it into three parts. In the first, we'll talk about knowing in community, particularly through the pastoral cohort model. In chapter 1, we discuss the exceptional benefit of the learning communities we developed in our pastoral cohorts. We'll also give you the tools to create your own or discern if you've found a good one. In chapter 2, we'll talk about the necessary parts of growth, particularly with your vocation. In chapter 3, we offer the model of a pastor as a political leader, which orients you toward your community in what might be an entirely new way.

The second part of the book directly addresses strategies for leadership in your community. Chapter 4 gives you strategies for learning in this new role and how to implement them in your context. Chapter 5 concerns the art of discernment amid all the new things you've learned and assumed in the role of a political leader. Chapter 6 provides methods of community engagement that make good use of what you have learned and discerned as a political leader. These include frameworks for approaching this work as well as concrete tools that come from those schools of thought. Chapter 7 leads you to do some serious reflection about your role in implementing these strategies and using the tactics we've described. We consider the idea of power and how pastors should and shouldn't use it.

We'll conclude the book with a final part to look at both the troubles and the joys of this community work. In chapter 8, we deal with the inevitable tension that comes from introducing potentially new or different ideas to your congregation. While this work is undoubtedly worth the cost, it is essential to understand the difficulties that accompany it. In the concluding chapter, we return to the absolute joy of a life in ministry and why your work matters.

While the writing of this book occasioned and furthered serious debates about ministry in community, one place where we are incorrigibly unanimous is our appreciation for the goodness of the work of parish ministry and the talented, faithful leaders who do it. Yes, it is hard, but it is also fun, a delight, and a joy, even. It is worth it. We strive to be worthy of the calling and hope that our book helps you to do the same.

PART I

Knowing in Community

1

Clergy Learning Communities

One of the co-authors of this book describes her experience with the pastoral leadership program as transformational: "When a pastor friend suggested I apply for the upcoming Fall pastor's learning cohort, he didn't even really describe what it was. Or I wasn't really listening. My experience with pastors' groups was limited, and the little I had seen didn't whip me into a ministerial frenzy. I just knew I needed to get out of my house, so I determined that if the big yellow bus did, in fact, pick up my children the first week of school (not having been again canceled by a fresh COVID-19 outbreak), I would hit send on my application. The bus came. As a result of those two years with a cohort of pastors who became not only colleagues but dear friends, a plethora of shared experiences transformed my understanding of parish life. I was introduced to books I never would have read on my own. And my memories continue to flash of countries visited, church spires, children's souvenirs made out of spent bullet casings, and octopus salads. My pastoral ministry will never be the same."

Part I. Knowing in Community

LEARNING IS AN ACT of bravery because it is an admission that we do not have all the answers. And we have less control than we might prefer in shaping the lessons that come to us. There is a very uncomfortable truth in the realization that we often do not even know what we don't know and thus have some reason to mistrust our intuitions of what we want to learn. For these and a thousand other reasons, finding ways of continued learning *with other peers* is vital, thrilling, and a way of healing from the many wounds and hurts a pastor experiences.

But how do you form a clergy community, join one, or find one? And what makes for a good one? The initiative of which we authors have been a part of for over a decade has supplied us with a great overview of clergy learning groups, and we want to tell you that what we have seen is worth seeking out to experience for yourself. In this book, we hope to give you a taste of that experience and offer you some of the most significant things we learned along the way.

Some pastors are guilted into or obligated to be a part of such a group. Denominational officials and church leadership boards encourage, and sometimes even require, pastors to participate in local ministeriums, peer learning groups, and clergy clusters. These can be of great value. Peer relationships with other clergy and vocational networks outside your church can provide meaningful social connection and mutual support in times of confusion and crisis. Yet, all groups are not equally impactful. Many lack a clear purpose or quickly devolve into gossip and gripe sessions. While these groups may provide a safe space for pastors to process a multiplicity of problems in the church, there are more meaningful ways for clergy to be in community with other clergy. When clergy participate in a distinctive pastoral learning community that gathers around a common mission and goal, the results buoy sagging spirits and bring fresh life to weary ministers. This is what happened at the fifteen institutions that comprised the Early Career Leadership Development Initiative. We have seen the powerful and positive impact and transformation this kind of group has had on pastors, their congregations, and their communities.

Unfortunately, many Christian denominations lack requirements for continuing education or professional learning communities of their clergy. Many pastors are not in a denominational accountability structure at all, because the polity to which they subscribe is strictly congregationalist without the oversight characteristic of other denominations. After their initial theological education in divinity school, Bible college, or seminary, pastors can coast for years, or even decades, without being exposed to new ways of doing ministry, new ideas, and new roles of leadership. Unless a pastor possesses a high level of self-motivation, they can hide behind the busyness of church life without any plan for personal or professional growth.

Before we dive into what we discovered and learned in our cohorts, we want to provide you with four characteristics that make a successful learning community: common purpose, diversity, covenants, and shared experiences.

COMMON PURPOSE

A learning group can be formed around a variety of shared purposes. What is most important is to give some careful consideration to what brings you together beyond your need for companionship. Any consistent gathering will bring you the companionship you seek—you need something else to make your clergy group successful. In our programs, we found that discussion, exposure, and teaching about the role of the pastor in their community was most effective (so that's what the rest of this book will be about). Part of the reason for that success is the shared point in the career arc of a pastor. In many (not all!) traditions, newly ordained clergy find themselves aware of and attentive to the particular stories, needs, and priorities of their local congregations rather than the communities in which those congregations are located. The same is, to a lesser but significant extent, true of pastors in new calls. It is congregation first, community second. However, it can be refreshing and energizing, after a period of familiarization with the congregation, to dig in and get to know the community.

Part I. Knowing in Community

Certainly, the social issues that clergy learning communities explored differed according to context, but the emphasis on leadership did not. Some focused on racism, immigration policy, and criminal justice reform. Others chose climate change, art, technology, good governance, or healthcare. Access to water is of vital concern in some contexts, whereas housing is far more important in others. In our common focus on civic engagement, we also emphasized the role of the pastor as the political leader, which we'll discuss in a later chapter. How broad or narrow your focus is depends on the interests of your group members and the salience of the moment in time. The purpose could be a variety of things, *but there really needs to be one.*

This shared purpose allows for the group members to grow alongside one another. It turns the gaze outward and thus helps to avoid the tendency to ruminate about the same old things. Rather than devolving into navel-gazing or gossip, the external focus provides a context for learning and growth. The clergy community then forms as a by-product of being in mission together, not the other way around. We are convinced that it is vital to have a common purpose so that for much of the time, the pastors are standing shoulder to shoulder rather than only face-to-face.

DIVERSITY

Another crucial component in an effective pastoral learning community is diversity. Learning is enhanced by encountering clergy of different racial and ethnic backgrounds, ecclesial traditions, genders, sexual orientations, socioeconomic status, and ministry settings. When clergy clusters are made up of people from the same race, ethnicity, or church type, it tends to reinforce presuppositions about ministry. But a pastoral learning community gathered with attention to diversity creates opportunities to understand issues from different vantage points. Together we learn to ask different and often better questions. Proverbs reminds us, "Iron sharpens iron, and one person sharpens the wits of another."[1] We see this truth come to life when diversity is part of the mix. What's more, if the learning group wants to do some work together with what they have learned, their work will have the credibility of having been born from diversity. In other words, it will be less likely to be suspected of being merely to the benefit of a particular few or inordinately shaped by one viewpoint to the exclusion of others.

Because there are so many external forms that differentiate human bodies, and internal forms that differentiate human minds, diversity should take account of many forms. Attention should be given to race, gender, class, ethnicity, age, place of origin, and formal education attainment. Some of our programs required a master's degree from an accredited school, and some did not. Some polities require such things, and others don't. Some denominations ordain women and LGBTQIA+ persons, and some do not. Our programs remain agnostic, for the most part, about criteria for inclusion or the *desiderata* of the makeup of the clergy learning community. But, like the existence of a shared common purpose, the commitment to diversity is vital.

Consider some examples:

> A group of pastors was reflecting on their conversation with a very established pastor in Dallas who led a successful organizing campaign in favor of public schools. He had encouraged them to recognize the power, prominence, and influence pastors still have when they walk into a legislator's office at the Texas State Capitol. In his experience, politicians stopped to listen when he started speaking, harkening back to an age where pastors were held in high esteem. He wanted the pastors in the group to claim their authority. But, very quickly into the group's reflection, several female members said, "Well, that may be true for the men here, but there's no way a woman has that much sway as a pastor. Sometimes we can't even get invited into the local ministerial alliances." Their perspective opened up a new line of inquiry for the group that had the male members asking how they could ally

---

1. Proverbs 27:17.

with their female colleagues to get them into the room. If there had not been women in the group, or if the women did not feel that they could voice their concerns, the conversation would not have been as rich.

Other kinds of difference matter, too. For example:

> In one of our cohorts, there was a large number of pastors from the same denomination, one in which the local bishop had a high degree of power to place pastors in calls. That denomination also required newer clergy to be in accountability groups. The pastors who later joined the clergy learning community that had a diverse array of denominations in it reflected on how hard their experience had been in the single-denomination group. They did not feel like they could really be honest about their struggles because they worried that their next posting (or lack of one) would suffer if word got out that they had made mistakes. No one wanted to make anyone else look bad, either, so discussions were anodyne and bland, a false peace could be kept, and the retreat would just end so people could get back to work.

Unless pastors have lived in various places, they can suffer from tunnel vision. The way a pastor approaches ministry in a secularized New England or Pacific Northwest context is very different from ministry in a Christian-saturated subculture in the American South or Midwest. Also, ministry in a middle-class rural village where people value preservation over progress is different from that in an affluent suburban development that is always emphasizing the next big thing. And both of these will differ from the ethos of an impoverished neighborhood in a large West Coast city like Los Angeles or San Francisco. Having an outsider's eyes on an insider culture can also help break open some of the long-standing areas of captivity or boredom that tend to become the wallpaper of our regional or cultural experience.

Pastoral expectations and pressures differ among churches of different sizes. Large churches value visionary pastors to set the course and tone for the pastoral staff and the whole congregation. This can produce a "grass is greener on the other side" dynamic.

For instance, a small church solo pastor may become discouraged by a constant lack of resources and loneliness in ministry, and desire to move into a larger church with a larger vision and more established programs. On the other hand, a large church pastor may be frustrated by the constant barrage of administrative duties and managing staff crises, and desire to shift to a smaller church with a more streamlined system and more opportunities to pray with people. When pastors of various-sized churches gather and learn together, it clarifies expectations and minimizes disillusionment.

COVENANTS

Another part of creating a compelling pastoral learning community is creating a safe space for intellectual honesty and personal vulnerability. You can craft that space by establishing some guidelines about treating everyone with respect and civility from the outset, such as a formal community covenant or shared agreement. Pastors need to know that all of their questions and ideas are welcomed at the table of conversation. Bringing a sense of humor is a must; pastors in a cohort need permission to take themselves lightly and the presence and mission of God seriously. Your covenant will ultimately be a creation of your group, but you should draft it at the beginning and call upon it when tension and disagreement arise.

The level of formality, scope of topics, and other features may well vary, and they may have to be somewhat fluid. One of our programs that began before 2010 required participants to sign a covenant of agreement that included a promise not to use any electronic devices during any session of the retreat. Such a stricture was already countercultural then, but it fairly quickly became untenable and unacceptable to the group. What is important is that members agree on what "full participation" means. If a clergy learning community is not important enough for the participants to prioritize, it probably is not worth having in that form.

A final element of agreements or covenants to consider is the duration of the community. Open-ended timelines invite a

Part I. Knowing in Community

petering out at the end and a lack of focus at the beginning. When the purpose is discovered and a diverse and committed group is formed, a frank discussion of goals and approaches that all endorse and know how to measure is appropriate and helpful. Some of these groups have resources, the expenditure of which determines the end of the group. Others don't have many resources aside from the pluck, commitment, and gifts of the participants.

Funding sources for these groups are far more numerous than one might think. Denominations and grant providers may come to mind. But there are many others to think about. Perhaps a group of pastors is growing concerned about climate change and water access. A college or university near them likely has academic departments with some expertise in such areas, and they also likely have "visiting speaker" committees eager to enrich the campus and surrounding community. If they were contacted by a group of pastors who asked, "Would you consider inviting a person to speak on this issue that many of us are organizing around?" then the results are very likely to be positive. Or perhaps a group of pastors is growing concerned about land use, development, and zoning. The decisions made by state and local governments affect the pastors' congregations and communities. But rarely are government employees asked respectfully for information, guidance, or other forms of support. Respect yourself enough to ask for resources that further your group's ends!

SHARED EXPERIENCES

The last characteristic of successful clergy learning communities is to do something besides having meetings. Developing a group bond or sense of cohesion is not automatic, but it will be accelerated by shared adventure. Entering into spaces together that are not "our spaces" can create a sense of vulnerability and provide a unique, mutual experience that aids in forming a bond. Pastors usually act as the expert or guide, but in a cohort model, they become learners together on a common journey. Spending both structured and unstructured time together over a series of days where there are shared meals, happy hours, and downtime can make room for relationships to grow.

The word *journey* in the paragraph above is used metaphorically, but a literal journey is perhaps the best adventure a clergy learning group can take. Such experiences can be expensive and difficult to manage from a logistical and time-sensitive point of view, but the payback is extraordinary. This experience is what puts pastors side by side and moves friendships forward. What's more, it is remarkable how much more clearly one can really "see" one's own context simply by leaving it and asking new questions about a place you know less well. One of our programs visited South Africa and learned about the church's role in opposing apartheid. The speakers were powerful, and the history lessons were accurate and carefully constructed. The real benefit for the pastors, however, was how it helped highlight similarities and differences in the United States' own legacy of racism and struggle for justice. Travel, in general, has this effect on many people, but there is something special about this particular kind of shared experience with members of your own profession, allies in your own learning community.

> Even during COVID-19, when one of our cohorts couldn't travel, they made their best effort to meet each other outside each other's church buildings. We sat outside the United Methodist Church in a rural town with a healthcare professional. We could physically see the healthcare clinic the church helped start. Literally in between the worship space and the clinic, we sat at the intersection between community concerns and the church. Another time, we sat outside in beautiful fall weather in a pristine, enclosed garden of an Episcopal church. The wealthy church sat in the middle of a mountain resort town. The priest was struggling to guide his congregation off their manicured lawn and into the rugged highlands where communities were suffering under the pressures of a housing shortage, food insecurity, and healthcare gaps. We could feel the disconnect ourselves by visiting his church grounds.

PART I. KNOWING IN COMMUNITY

WHAT WE LEARNED TOGETHER

One of us co-authors grew up on a farm almost entirely surrounded by a stream. As a boy, he tried to arrange stepping stones at strategic points where he wanted to get across the stream without getting wet, but had to keep rebuilding them as they washed away. He noticed something about walking across these improvised bridges. You could never stay on one stone too long. You needed some momentum and you had to keep going. The stones were tippy and their footing fragile, but they sustained a walker better than a stander. Philosophers might call that a dialectic, but the main thing is the alternation. Left foot, right foot, left foot, right foot.

The dialectic you'll see unfold in this book is between companion and leader. A companion is someone who eats bread with you. Com = with and pan = bread. Clergy are pulled into isolation in so many ways by so many forces, but multiple layers of community can serve as countervailing forces. Whether it's a clergy learning group, a local congregation, or a group of civic leaders, we hope to see pastors who are and who have companions. They may be eucharistic companions in the best case: pastors willing to share in life together for mutual sustenance. After all, to borrow Martin Luther's earthy phrase, a Christian is just one beggar showing another beggar where to find some bread.

Our clergy cohorts across vast geographies and experiences of the participants taught us some unifying things—bread we found that we'd like to share. The central theme that ran through our various experiences was leadership. Our pastors confront a significantly different cultural reality now than they would have ten, twenty, or thirty years ago. How does a pastor lead now? What does the pastor's life look like now? The rest of this book will consider answers to those questions. We'll propose to you a model of pastoral ministry and the tools needed to make it work. Whatever point you're at in your ministerial career, or if you're just considering a career in ministry, we hope the qualities, methods, and perspectives on leadership will energize or clarify your own calling as a pastor. Before we turn to them, we need to consider what it will mean for you to change and grow as a pastor.

2

Growing Leadership Capacities

THE FIRST QUALITY ANY pastoral leader needs is the capacity for growth. Stagnation is not an option in ministry. It can be severely injurious to you and your congregation if, all the way to the end of your career, you retain the same habits, strategies, and perspectives you had when you first left seminary.

The need for growth may seem common sense, bordering on a useless statement, but many pastors neglect their own growth while attending to that of others. Often pastors commit this error because they understand that growth requires some tough stuff, and they're not ready for it. Perhaps they'd rather avoid it entirely.

Every metaphor is partial, and every image or model of how to think about pastoral leadership is incomplete. As one of our daughters reminded us, "Like means *unlike*." When we say something is like something else, we also mean it's not like it, too. Here, we want you to consider the life of the community-based pastor as a kind of tree in a forest. Trees appear to us as individual organisms, but they are, through their rootedness, deeply communal. Consider the colony of Pando, a large organism of aspens in southwest Utah. Possessing a single genome, this organism, which looks from afar to be a series of different trees, spans 107 acres. Rather than a common forest, it is potentially the largest single-species organism in the world. Pastors should take heed of that rooted communal life because while they may seem like individuals, they are deeply enmeshed in a community and cannot exist apart from it. Further, the more deeply rooted a pastor becomes, the more potential there is for growth.

This growth will require patience, curiosity, often discomfort, and always change. The pastor, the congregation, and the community itself may prefer stasis but it's not sustainable. It's a natural thing and a neutral observation to say the status quo is preferable to all these parties. However, the pastor especially will find that in the absence of growth, the plant will wither.

THE PAIN OF GROWTH

Like trees, pastors will invariably experience woundedness throughout their lifetime. Whether it's a tree or a pastor, either one can be harmed by environmental conditions, premature pruning, constricting placement, or invasive insects. Sometimes these wounds run so deep that they even cause pastors to question their vocational call. Early career pastors are especially vulnerable to these threats. It takes time to grow a thick enough bark that one can endure this pain. At the same time, even when you've been somewhere a long time, the pain can still surprise you and catch you off guard. Sometimes, the longer you've been somewhere, the more the pain will hurt when it gets through the bark.

> When one of our clergy cohorts from New England took a trip to the Balkans, the travelers met with local pastors and church leaders to learn about issues such as religious identity, racial tensions, nationalism, and the effects of war and genocide. One day, the cohort found themselves engaged in an intense conversation at a cemetery in Mostar, Herzegovina. Even though the city's majestic sixteenth-century Ottoman architecture has been largely restored, it still bore the physical and emotional scars from the war. The group's members couldn't help but notice the bullet holes and hollow spaces in many of the buildings across the street and that all of the white gravestones were marked with death dates between

Part I. Knowing in Community

1991 and 1995. Karmelo, a pastor who lived through the war in that place, shared the haunting story of how city parks, throughout Bosnia and Herzegovina, had been converted to cemeteries during the war. When one of the cohort members asked how the younger generation was handling the lingering trauma, Pastor Karmelo gazed across the young trees growing in the graveyard, and then he whispered, "We probably all have PTSD. We've just learned to live with it."

The good news is that wounds can be healed and produce even greater growth. We inevitably learn to live with pain, but how we do so is critical. Henri Nouwen, in his influential book *The Wounded Healer*,[1] teaches pastors how. Few of us enjoy pain, but when we reflect on our lives, how many times have we experienced goodness that we would have never encountered except for the trials that preceded it? James reminds us, "My brothers and sisters, whenever you face trials of any kind, consider it nothing but joy, because you know that the testing of your faith produces endurance; and let endurance have its full effect, so that you may be mature and complete, lacking in nothing."[2] Woundedness can serve as a source of strength and healing when ministering to others. That doesn't make the original pain justifiable or dismissible; rather, we can sometimes transform our pain into something that helps even in the hurt.

Consider again the wisdom of a tree when tending to our woundedness. Trees are wounded in many ways, including constriction, rough pruning, or invasive predation. All of these wounds as experienced by the pastor, can be powerfully tended in a cohort of colleagues. Far from gripe sessions that further alienate us from the necessary work at hand, we found most healing cohorts of colleagues who were candid, humorous, and careful thinkers, with each pastor that experienced one of these three kinds of woundedness.

Like the tree that is planted within the design of a sidewalk, the constricted space for a pastor seems a dead end for far-reaching

---

1. Nouwen, *Wounded Healer*, especially chapter 4.
2. James 1:2–4.

ministry. The constriction can come from congregational anxiety, lack of rapport in the community, doctrines, or denominational policies. The technique of a tree is to go deeper first and reach under the restrictions in order to empower the canopy. In this way, pastors may receive a cue to attend to their rootedness to overcome constriction. You may need to grow down before you can grow up and out. Consider attending to the capacities, skills, and history of your congregation as a way to build trust, experience, and assets for your own growth. Those present gifts may be the key to moving in the direction a pastor wants to go. Likewise, your clergy cohort may be rich soil for your roots, providing support emotionally, materially, and creatively for your ministry in times of constraint.

Trees never know when someone is going to prune them. Rough pruning never feels fair. It comes out of nowhere and can easily take a pastor out of commission. We experience a loss of opportunity, resources, and reach. Just when an arm of ministry was growing so beautifully, it was lopped off from its vitality by the loss of a gift or a person from the congregation. In such moments, the technique of the tree is to seal off the wound so that invasive energy cannot enter the tree. This allows for a time of recovery and redirected growth. As a pastor, you can acknowledge the wound and reassess your circumstances without allowing the wound site to put everything at risk. Consulting your colleagues about your pain in this area can both yield new ideas and properly contextualize your pain. Diversity in your pastoral ecosystem is vital here as those in different contexts can provide new avenues and perspectives you don't have access to on your own. With the contrast in their roles and contexts, a Black pastor serving a politically active church downtown may have different ideas about how to address a problem or failure than a White pastor at a small rural congregation.

Trees and pastors know something about predators. They are gnawing and nibbling through the bark toward what we hold precious. Maybe it's a church member who's found exactly what buttons to press, a community member who wants to sabotage the congregation's efforts, or an event in your own life that's threatening to derail your ministry. The trees' techniques for response include surface detours such as thick bark, thorns, or leaf hairs. With all this, the most effective technique is a change at the cellular level that resists decay or creates material that is indigestible by predators. This might be characterized as deep work. There are nibbling rumors and gnawing gossip that waft about in the pastor's life. This reality stings and wounds a pastor and, if left unattended, can infiltrate the mind, psyche, and behavior. Deep work, in this instance, might include a prayer that intends not to villainize those who participate in rumor or gossip but to compassionately hold them to account if there is a right moment. And until then, a detoxifying prayer may help, such as, "This hurts me, and it hurts me a lot, but may I experience strength as I move through it toward the strength of the community."

THE PATIENCE OF GROWTH

Time with our cohorts can slow us down in invaluable ways, as Tolkien's Ents insist, "We never say anything unless it is worth taking a long time to say."[3] Don't forget, the coming of the kingdom of God is far more often compared to something which grows so slowly that the natural eye might not even perceive it, like seeds that grow and bread that rises. There simply is no fast food for those who hunger and thirst for righteousness. But there is daily bread. Within the rhythms of each day, if the pastor embraces patience, they can gather their sustenance from the imperfect systems that surround them. Amid the hospital visitation, a pastor can be inspired by the collaboration of doctors and nurses as well as the tear that slides down a patient's cheek following a prayer. During a city council meeting, the pastor can find wonder at the number of citizens who have gathered to share concern and passion over the shared life of a community. In providing a bag of food to a passing stranger, the pastor may be humbled as that stranger shares their food with another "rough sleeper."[4] When we might otherwise be

---

3. Tolkien, *Two Towers*, bk. 3, ch. 4.
4. See Kidder, *Rough Sleepers*, ch. 5.

weighed down by more tenacious frustrations, even injustices that threaten to infect us with a fatalistic cynicism, these moments of patient attention allow us to experience glimpses of the often invisible connections between us all.

Pastors are often on the receiving end of transference and projection by their parishioners. Navigating through proverbial minefields of spoken and unspoken expectations is one of the greatest demands within congregational life. This, coupled with pastors' unrealistic expectations of themselves, can create standards that can domesticate a pastor toward "playing it safe" in the life of the parish. Patience to create a culture in which experimentation is valued and mistakes are honored can contribute to a pastor's well-being and that of the congregation. The trust we most need is perhaps the trust we can first give by observing and listening to our parishioners. Sometimes they have many clues that will further congregational life. Learning about and honoring their competencies can create terrific momentum for their capacity to honor their pastor in authentic ways. We have to be patient enough to do that hard work.

If there are expectations within the walls, there can be suspicions outside the walls in the byways of public life. Suspicions rise between faith traditions across denominations, races, and genders. Pastors can be looked upon with nostalgia or resentment. Gone are the days when pastors were venerated by virtue of their position. Surely in part due to religious scandals of abuse, theological hypocrisy in our practices, or untenable assertions within our doctrines, there is a distrust of church and clergy. Ascribed honor to clergy has dropped off dramatically. Pastors, whether it is justified or not, are in a position of need to earn trust and maybe some honor along with it.

For the most part, the vocations of science and medicine have assumed the authority to interpret life, death, and the meaning that lies between them. So, the work is rather exhausting to earn our cultural place as interpreters of life and life abundant. Like the slow and patient growth of a tree, our work to develop trust with our communities inside and outside the walls of our church building can be some of the slowest work of ministry. Nevertheless, it is vital for growing our competencies, capabilities, and influence. If we can rise to these challenges in pastoral life, we can find it benefits not just the tree that is ourselves but the whole forest that is our congregation and community.

GROWTH AS CHANGE

Beyond the pain and patience that growth requires, the most fundamental effect is change. A tree in its early growth stages doesn't just look like a small version of its mature self. Likewise, all of our pastors acknowledged that they could not continue in their ministry without change, either in themselves, in their environments, or both. To develop a capacity for change, there are several things you can keep in mind.

First and foremost, curiosity and wonder make change possible. Jesus reminds us of this when he tells us, "Truly I tell you, unless you change and become like children, you will never enter the Kingdom of Heaven."[5] Often we reserve the quality of wonder for children and sometimes for the older creative types, but wonder is a necessity for all of us even to imagine that the world could be different. Each of us is built for wonder, and we must resist modern life's attempts to push us away from it. After all, Socrates was often quoted saying, "Wisdom begins in wonder."

In the same way, curiosity must routinely get the best of you if you want to grow. Many of the techniques and exercises we will introduce to you in the following chapters assume a posture of curiosity. Your vocation will only survive if you are curious about how it might shift and change with time. You can't afford to be bound to how you expected ministry to be so much that you miss what ministry actually is.

Play is another thing usually reserved for children and only, at best, occasionally indulged by adults (and even then, often only in the company of children). Be playful with your sense of vocation and the strictures of your role. Don't take them so seriously

---

5. Matthew 18:3.

that you snuff the life out of them. Experimentation and play will open up new avenues for growth for you and your congregation.

Lest these ideas lull you into a false sense of security about this work, know that ministry also requires a great deal of resiliency. The capacity for toughness and snapping back after difficult circumstances is part of the way our physical body finds its strength. When our muscles are put under appropriate strain and stress, our strength and our agility can improve. Or, to continue the forest metaphor, trees need practice in resisting prevailing winds. When smaller, younger trees are partially sheltered from strong winds by a stout mature tree, the fibers in their lower trunks become brittle because they do not have to "practice" pushing back. When the mature tree dies, the younger ones are easily toppled in subsequent years. There is an exhilaration that comes through hardship. That does not justify the hard time that we go through, but staying mindful of the byproduct as a potential benefit is yet another way to honor yourself and your vocation.

For any of the following chapters to make sense, you must be open to change. To make that change last, you need to maintain these qualities, as well. It's one thing to become so excited about an idea on a retreat with your cohort and quite another to implement it in your community, which naturally prefers stasis.

Your capacity for change is what allows your identity to shift and new aspects of yourself to emerge. Our cohorts held a transformative power in increasing our capacity for and openness to this kind of change. One set of our cohorts began their sessions with inventories of self-understanding. One of the questions asked the participants how much they saw themselves as a political leader at the beginning of the program, and they asked the same question at the end. The share of participants that said they saw themselves as political leaders increased substantially throughout the program, marking an emerging identity many of the pastors discovered over their time in their cohort. Given the consistency of this identity emerging in our cohorts, we now turn to what we discovered it meant to be a pastor as a political leader.

3

Pastor as Political Leader

As we analyzed what created the transformative power for our clergy who intentionally engaged in the multiple layers of community around them, we realized that their particular role of leadership was key. We invite you to consider a different way of looking at your role as a pastor: as a political leader. Why use the term *political* when it carries such a charge? Even at this moment, you may be able to hear the voice of a congregation member saying, "Pastors should stay out of politics!" You may bristle at the idea of commingling ministry and politics. We suggest the term "political leader," in part, to provoke you to think about what you are doing when you step into the public square in a leadership capacity.[1]

Of course, as a pastor, you may already see yourself as a political leader and recognize no controversy at all in taking on this role. Our unique social location determines our lens and perspective. "An individual's social location is defined as the combination of factors including gender, race, social class, age, ability, religion, sexual orientation, and geographic location. This makes social

---

1. As a collaborative group of authors from diverse backgrounds, we debated the use of the word *political*, and decided to keep it despite the complex ways that it landed for each of us. We thought there might be something important in the term precisely because it landed awkwardly for our group and stirred debate.

location particular to each individual; that is, social location is not always exactly the same for any two individuals."[2] For example, many BIPOC pastors in the South find they are required to take on a public role. They have been called to the congregation in order to solve the community's problems through politics. To divorce political and pastoral would be inauthentic to the role churches have played in fighting injustice in their communities since the United States was formed. Similarly, many BIPOC pastors serving on reservations feel their role requires political engagement for the very survival of their congregants. They cannot be absent from politics lest their community's voice be erased from the conversation entirely.

Even if your congregation expects you to be a political leader, you may not feel equipped for that role. You may have had little opportunity for serious reflection or preparation in this capacity. Some pastors find their expected level of political engagement leaves them little time for pastoral care, theological reflection, and casual conversation.

This chapter is for you, no matter how you identify with the pastor as a "political leader." We think that phrase can help illuminate important dimensions of a pastoral vocation that extends into the community beyond the congregation and pastors across contexts and initial predispositions.

WHY POLITICAL?

Politics is not simply the bickering on cable news or the partisan mudslinging everyone seems to do but no one claims to like. Instead, politics is ultimately about how we live together and how we make decisions together. It's how we do *life together*, to borrow Bonhoeffer's phrase again. At this very basic level, then, a political leader is someone who guides, directs, or influences the relations of a community, whether it be a small church, a township, or a nation. In this sense, a pastor is already acting as a political leader

2. National Council on Family Relations, "Inclusion and Diversity Committee Report."

Part I. Knowing in Community

in their congregation. For most people, however, the term *politics* almost exclusively conjures systems of governance common to people living within a particular geographical boundary (city, county, state, nation). It involves elections, elected officials, political parties, and therefore disagreement and divisiveness. Also, politics always involves power. And power makes a lot of Christians uncomfortable.

Despite, and perhaps because of these misgivings, we want to reclaim the word *political* as descriptive of a pastor's call—to seek peace, to work for the good of the whole community, and to use power in life-giving ways. Consider the words of the prophet Jeremiah, "But seek the well-being of the city where I have sent you into exile, and pray to the Lord on its behalf, for in its welfare you will find your welfare."[3] We see from this passage that the well-being of Judean exiles is intertwined with the well-being of Babylon. The exiles' dependence on Babylon, however, is not the only reason God will watch out for the city. Judah is learning that God is sovereign over history, not just current events in Palestine. The exiles can trust that in working for the good of the city, they are doing a just and holy thing in obedience to God.[4]

There is a temptation for both the pastor and the congregation to see themselves as separate from the "community." While congregations might have distinct ways of relating and responding, they are nevertheless nested within the greater ecology of their city or town. In the community ecology, lives are intertwined and mutually interdependent. As Martin Luther King Jr. said in his "Letter from a Birmingham Jail," "We are caught in an inescapable network of mutuality, tied in a single garment of destiny. Whatever affects one directly, affects all indirectly."[5] The pastor as a political leader recognizes this invisible web of relationships and it fundamentally reorients their perspective from the caretaker of a congregation to a leader in a community of which the

---

3. Jeremiah 29:7.

4. "Obedience" is sometimes unfashionable as a model of the Christian life. Its etymology comes from *ob-audiens*, a particularly intense form of listening.

5. King Jr., "Letter from a Birmingham Jail," 75.

congregation is a part. The congregation is inherently political by its very nature. When we recognize that the congregation is part of a political community, the whole of that community becomes the pastor's parish.

COMMUNITY AS PARISH

We believe that this move toward thinking about the community as a parish can bring reinvigoration to your sense of call. Focusing your energy primarily on your congregation can be both isolating and limiting. If you have ever felt a disconnect between your regular activities and the passion that led you into ministry, it may be time to enlarge your idea of whom you are called to serve. We think that making this shift can move you in a life-giving direction because it brings your ministry into greater alignment with God's call to seek the well-being of the city. It also repeats the patterns in the ministry of Jesus, who did not spend time solely in the temple. Jesus was out among the people, meeting the Samaritan woman at the well, traveling toward the centurion's home, and addressing the crowd by the Sea of Galilee. Likewise, the apostle Paul traveled not only to speak in synagogues but spoke in public spaces to public leaders, such as at the Areopagus in Athens.[6] While the content and style of a pastor's speech in public might differ today from Paul's rhetoric, the key point is that a pastor's place is not confined to a subset of people nor to a church building.

The move into greater awareness of and intentional engagement in the community ecology is not only invigorating for the life of the pastor but also for the life of the congregation. When the church sees itself as a participant in a larger whole, it does not have to keep recreating energy to sustain itself solely within itself. The church, as it seeks the well-being of the whole community, increases its own well-being.

---

6. Acts 17:16–31.

Part I. Knowing in Community

THE CHURCH'S DISTINCTIVE GIFTS FOR THE COMMUNITY

Pastors and churches bring a distinct, if not unique, angle when addressing problems within a community. The ends Christians seek may well be nuanced differently—shalom for all rather than particular outcomes like electoral results or unfettered growth. Likewise, the means Christians endorse and use may well be different—peaceful rather than dominating or destructive. But most importantly, the motivations that Christians bring will be different. Understood in biblical context, Christian work for the city where you live is obedience to the command of God to work for the dignity of all.

The church, too, is a unique entity in the political life of a community. There's something different about a church community from a Rotary Club, Lion's Club, or even from social services and nonprofit organizations. If the church merely wanted the same things by the same means as other political groups, why bother becoming a pastor when you could just run for mayor instead?

In the 1910s, Swiss theologian Karl Barth recognized that the church in which he served was largely conceding its imagination to nonsectarian structures and institutions. The church is fundamentally different because of its transcendent claims and its relationship with a God who is more dynamic and even demanding than our own idealized versions of ourselves. Encounter with God can revolutionize how the pastor approaches being a political leader and how the church understands itself as part of a political community. Barth exemplified this in his approach to his parish. In addition to his usual tasks of preaching, visiting, and teaching confirmation classes, as a pastor, he engaged in such community activities as leading the Blue Cross Temperance Society, conducting the Blue Cross choir, teaching classes on science, personal hygiene, bookkeeping, and coaching girls sports.[7]

The church, after all, attends to transcendent beauty and righteousness and not just the means of production, shuffling of

---

7. Busch, *Karl Barth*, 65–67.

capital, and concern for worldly hierarchies. The belief that God is not absent from any aspect of human life can infuse our relationships, our art, and our political lives with beauty beyond what is immediately expedient. When the church looks at affordable housing, for example, the pastor and members should not just advocate for the cheapest solution to house the most people but be attentive to the thriving and dignity of the people who will live there. One of us working on an affordable housing project encountered an architect driven by this vision, and every design he made held the human experience of the residents as the first priority. People who need housing deserve dignity and beauty as much as those who are already housed. That concern is not the sole province of the church, but it should be a particular concern.

When churches embrace this holy attention in their life together in the community, our churches become welcoming homes and safe harbors for all people. The belonging and inclusion that all of us crave can be generated in our beloved communities of dignity and beauty. Unbound from the specific concerns of production and capital, churches can fill their communities with life and beauty.

> One of the co-authors felt a specific call from God to participate in a local initiative where families provided crisis housing for children. At first, she and her husband thought it was an odd thing for a pastor to do, especially a pastor with several small children of their own. However, as they learned more about the overwhelmed foster care system in their region, they saw how vital this stopgap was for the children and the community. A mother and four-year-old daughter came to live with the pastor, and the child stayed with them while her mother gave birth to her sister. Because of the specific concern for these people that exceeded the bounds of government or commerce, the relationship became so much more. The whole church rallied around the child with medical attention, toys, and other necessities. They gathered around the mother and prayed for her, playing a pivotal role in her liberation from her addiction. From that point on, the pastor's congregation engaged in the foster care

crisis deeply and personally, choosing among themselves to adopt, sponsor, or otherwise support children in need in their community.

THE NEED FOR PROXIMITY

The closeness of the pastor, congregation, and community is vital for the pastor as a political leader. You cannot expect to understand, represent, or change your community if you are not proximate to it. Founder of the Equal Justice Initiative Bryan Stevenson insists, "You cannot be an effective problem-solver from a distance. There are details and nuances that you will miss unless you are close enough to observe those details." And, "If you are willing to get closer to the people who are suffering, you will find the power to change the world."[8] Proximity is a critical ingredient for change and for a healthy life together that both pastors and congregations often miss. If the congregation segregates itself from the rest of the community by lines of class, race, geography, or any other characteristic, it removes itself from the concerns of the community. The social fabric frays because concerns cease to be shared among the whole community. When those within the walls of the church (including the pastor) don't share the concerns of those outside the walls, the distance grows between them, far exceeding what their geography might suggest. At that moment, you lose proximity. And the more we distance ourselves from the crises our communities face, the less equipped we are to confront those problems alongside our church members and our neighbors.

Jesus, in particular, was insistent on this proximity. "Bring them to me" is a consistent refrain. When the disciples fear that they don't have enough to feed the thousands following Jesus, he says, "Bring them here to me," and in nearness to them, feeds them.[9] After the transfiguration, when the disciples are unable to help a young boy in distress, Jesus says, "Bring him to me."[10] When

8. Fernandez, "Empathy and Social Justice."
9. Matthew 14:18.
10. Mark 9:19.

desperate friends interrupt his teaching and lower a man through the roof, Jesus doesn't send them away; instead, he brings himself to the man and heals his paralysis.[11] When the disciples try to dismiss children as disruptive to his ministry, Jesus welcomes them, "Let the children come to me."[12] When the ostracized woman bleeding internally reaches out to touch him, Jesus doesn't send her away but honors her faith amid the community that shunned her.[13] Proximity was key.

CULTIVATION OF RELATIONSHIPS

Being close to suffering and crisis as a leader requires relationships, including ones the pastor might not traditionally embrace. The pastor, as a political leader, should embrace relationships with people in all parts of the political body. The recipients of benevolence ideally have a relationship with the pastor rather than just receiving temporary material assistance. They may even become part of the congregational community, where their proximity can't be ignored. Pastors as political leaders should also pursue relationships with those at the other end of our social hierarchies—the ones with decision-making capacities and power of their own. The purpose, however, is not to hobnob or ingratiate yourself with powerful people. Instead, you want to serve as a conversation partner, a source of conviction and pressure, and a voice for the interests you and your community share.

All of these relationships have different dimensions. The careful pastor, as a political leader, maintains both public and private relationships. Typically, everyone enjoys private relationships with people like their friends and family and public relationships with people like employers, the principal of a child's school, or perhaps other business colleagues. These relationships differ profoundly in their purpose and expectations. In a private relationship, you

---

11. Luke 5:17–26 (cf. Matthew 9:1–8, Mark 2:1–12).
12. Matthew 19:14; Mark 10:14; Luke 18:16.
13. Mark 5:25–34; Luke 8:43–48.

Part I. Knowing in Community

share in vulnerability, mutual support, and often candor. In a public relationship, you may be friendly but each party has aims, goals, and agendas they want to accomplish. Lest that seem strange, some common purposes of public relationships might include the well-being of your child at school (a public relationship with their teacher), a request for a raise or other change in compensation (a public relationship with your employer), or competition over customers (a public relationship between business owners).

The pastor as a political leader acknowledges that not only do they have both of these kinds of relationships, but they often have both kinds of relationships with the same individual. One of the key relationships that the pastor as a political leader can and should develop is with other civic leaders. Politicians, government officials, and local business leaders are obvious candidates for a public relationship but not off limits from a private one, as well. Both relationships are valuable and can help a pastor learn new things, accomplish objectives, and strengthen the network of relationships in their community.

> One of us has become good friends with multiple city council members in our town. The pastor and the council members share some common goals and policy preferences but also frequently speak together as friends. The pastor, however, is careful to maintain clear boundaries in those relationships because the occasion may arise in which they aren't on the same side on a given issue. If the pastor were to be advocating for an ecological policy that the council members opposed, a strong private relationship cannot stand in the way of the necessities of the public relationship. Familiarity cannot dull the pastor's commitment to the community's needs. Differentiation and boundaries are essential. Community organizers frequently remind us that there are no permanent enemies and no permanent allies. Maintaining these multiple levels of relationship ensures an enduring connection that survives public conflict.

Relationships with other civic leaders aren't always about navigating conflict, however. The pastor as a political leader would be wise to open themselves up to learning from these new friends (or foes), as well. Government officials can teach pastors about the functions of the bureaucracies in their municipalities and how the levers of power actually relate to one another. Business leaders can explain the constraints and possibilities they deal with regularly. Hospital administrators, doctors, and nurses can help you understand the healthcare challenges and opportunities in your area. Frequently, people are eager to share their knowledge, and that knowledge may be essential to addressing the needs of your community. In the ideal scenario, this becomes a two-way street where the pastor and other community leaders share their knowledge, holding space to expand each other's worlds.

In that spirit, one of us embraced their municipality's overt efforts to educate local leaders on the inner workings of government. Along with a cohort of other local leaders, the pastor went through a crash course in town government where they met key decision-makers who don't make headlines and powerful people who do jobs that don't wind up on the ballot. The relationships and knowledge developed in this process provided the avenues the pastor needed to later pursue affordable housing projects. When it came time to propose these projects to the local government, there were already multiple people interested, invested, and intrigued by the project. None of that would have happened without the public relationships built into that process, regardless of the quality of the housing proposal.

QUALITIES TO DEVELOP

Something we hope has become apparent in this sketch of the pastor as a political leader is the need for some essential qualities: curiosity and adaptability. Over the next several chapters, we hope to expose you to ways in which the pastor as a political leader can engage and develop those qualities. The pastor must be open to continual learning and possess the humility to admit that there's always more that they don't know. With all the learning the pastor does and all the needs pastors are exposed to in their communities,

Part I. Knowing in Community

discernment of how to use their limited time and resources is essential. Having a diverse range of responses to these needs you've learned about will make accomplishing your goals more attainable. Finally, the pastor must engage in reflection on their role and their power in the systems that both create and solve problems. A cohort of fellow clergy provides a safe and knowledgeable space to reflect on your own curiosity and adaptability.

These disciplines are more stances than stages. Rather than a linear process, consider it more like a labyrinth divided into four quadrants. The labyrinth weaves back in on itself repeatedly, and on the way to the center, you enter and exit the quadrants over and over again. Unlike the labyrinth, which has a final center, the pastor never ceases movement between these stances: learning, discerning, responding, and reflecting.

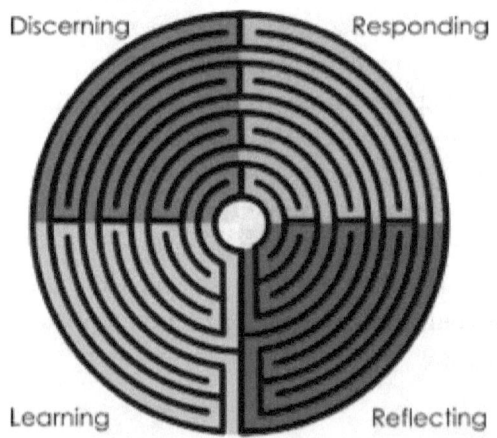

In addition to curiosity and adaptability, another essential quality for becoming a political leader is courage. There is great risk involved in this ambitious endeavor, and it can produce considerable fear on the part of the pastor, congregation, or community. Fears of criticism and failure abound, but just as Joshua found courage in the Lord's presence to lead the Israelites over the Jordan River to take possession of the land that God had promised them, we hope pastors will hear the echoes of God's voice resounding, "I hereby command you: Be strong and courageous; do not be frightened or dismayed, for the LORD your God is with you where you go."[14] Leadership always requires courage, but this is especially true when the stakes are high.

> A pastor in one of our cohorts took an enormous risk when he planned a special commissioning service at his church for the whole delegation of county legislators. After calming fears and gaining consensus from his church leadership board, he wrote personalized invitations to each legislator (Republicans and Democrats) and explained that the purpose of the service was to thank the legislators for their service to the community and to pray for them as they entered a new congressional session. No posturing, and no partisan agendas! As it turned out, ten of the twelve legislators attended the service and many curious townsfolk showed up for the event. Everyone recited liturgies and sang hymns together. The pastor preached a meaningful sermon from 1 Timothy 2:1–7 about the importance of praying for people who God has placed in high positions. And the church elder board called the legislators to the front of the church, laid hands on them, and prayed for them one by one. It was a powerful moment of civility and sacramental love. And as parishioners and politicians drank coffee and ate muffins in the fellowship hall after the service, everyone agreed that the event was a resounding success. Several legislators were moved to tears and asked if this could become an annual event. And they thanked the pastor for having the courage to execute such an audacious idea.

As pastors grow in their ability to be curious, adaptable, and courageous, they will be in a better position to become political leaders in their congregations and communities. As we mentioned at the beginning of this chapter, pastors are not necessarily politicians, but we hope that you will become curious enough to look beyond the walls of your office and see the possibilities around you. We hope that you will become adaptable enough to change directions when it is required. And we hope that you will become courageous enough to embrace the risk of becoming a pastor who

14. Joshua 1:9.

is considered a political leader. But if a pastor is to ever become this type of leader, there is still so much to learn.

PART II

Leading in Community

4

Learning the Layers of Your Community

Learning

THE FIRST ESSENTIAL ACTIVITY of the pastor as a political leader is learning. Learning leads to clergy seeing the transformational power that comes from intentionally engaging the multiple layers of community around them. While that may seem intuitive, pastors need to deliberately engage in this activity, not just assume they are passively learning. How you learn and change over time helps inform how you conceive of the various stages of your

Part II. Leading in Community

ministry career. It can be helpful to think of learning as something that exists along a developmental continuum that you traverse throughout the life of ministry. Knowing something about the developmental journey toward acquiring expertise as a pastor can help normalize your current position and help you see where you are going next. In this chapter, we want to begin by looking at a particular framework for adult learning that applies to you as a pastor and then move on to how you learn specifically about your congregation and community.

In 1980, educators Bert and Stuart Dreyfus articulated a now widely accepted theory of adult skill acquisition that proposes a continuum where one progresses from novice to expert. As a novice learner, you acquire knowledge and skill rather indiscriminately or context-free and are highly analytical in your process. As you progress along the developmental continuum, you grow in both your complexity and judgment. As you advance to the proficient stage, your learning becomes more situational, your perspective more experienced, and your commitment to acquiring a skill or knowledge more involved. Only when you reach the expert stage does your process of learning become truly intuitive and integrated.

Our experience is that most mid-career pastors (five to fifteen years in ministry) fall somewhere in the middle of the learning continuum. They are competent in the basic rhythms of their role, whether that be preaching a weekly sermon or making pastoral visits to congregational members. However, the shift in skill levels, knowledge, and perspective as early career pastors become mid-career pastors can be frustrating. For instance, an early career pastor's lack of skill can create a sense of urgency where you find yourself saying things like: "Oh gosh, I hope I can pull a sermon together before midnight . . ." If the sermon is preached well, it produces a sense of satisfaction. But as your skills improve and you become aware of a wider variety of homiletical approaches, the process becomes more complicated and perhaps less satisfying. Eventually, you have to decide which approach to adopt or attempt them all, which often leads to increased confusion and decreased confidence. Either way, greater awareness often leads to greater frustration.

The shift from detached understanding to involved understanding at this stage of your ministry can lead to a similar disillusionment. Beginning pastors expect to make mistakes in ministry, and they are often more merciful to themselves when something doesn't go well. But as a pastor grows in knowledge and skill, expectations increase internally and externally (from the congregation). We find that pastors solve their frustration by going in one of two directions: either they continue to embrace the challenge of adaptation and growth or they become entrenched in the status quo and insist: "This is just who I am" or "This is the way I do it."

If ever there was an injunction against settling for the status quo, it is found in an obscure (and ironic) verse in Luke's Gospel. After Luke recounts the story of a twelve-year-old Jesus slipping away from his parents to teach the teachers of the Law at the temple in Jerusalem, he inserts this seemingly minor detail, "And Jesus increased in wisdom and in years, and in divine and human favor."[15] But if Jesus, as God in human flesh, needed to learn and grow in intellectual wisdom, physical stature, spiritual insight, and social acumen, how much more does the rest of humanity need to do so? Luke was quite intentional about highlighting Jesus' holistic human development for the benefit of his readers. This verse, as well as the similar one in Luke 2:40, compels us to keep learning and sharpening our skills.

We invite you to embrace challenge and adaptation as your path. As you keep learning and growing toward expertise, you will find that intuition eventually replaces analytic decision-making. The detached nature of deciding gives way to full involvement and commitment. Our shared hope is that your resilience in this pursuit will lead you through the dark night of the soul in ministry, and you will find the dawning of your expertise beautiful to behold. The consistency and diversity of a clergy cohort can play a critical role in developing that resiliency through the support and challenge of your colleagues. In that context, we believe that one

15. Luke 2:52.

Part II. Leading in Community

highly effective way to keep growing as a pastor is to keep developing yourself as a pastor who is a political leader.

As you grow in self-awareness and gain confidence in embracing the role of pastor as political leader, it is important to learn about the congregation you're leading and for them to gain a better understanding of themselves. If there isn't shared clarity about where the congregation has been in the past—its triumphs, strengths, vulnerabilities, and weaknesses—it's difficult to know what to celebrate, which issues need to be treated with special sensitivity, and where the church is poised to serve the community. This journey of exploration and discovery can be embarked upon together. A great place to begin is cultivating the art of listening.

LISTENING

Listening involves the avoidance of presumptions and an openness to new information. Coming into a congregation or even having been in a congregation for a long time naturally leads us to operate based on simplistic heuristics, stereotypes, or assumptions to fill in our gaps in knowledge. The pastor needs to learn their own biases in these directions to avoid a failure to listen. What you think you know about someone in your congregation may not be the whole picture. Here is where pastors would be wise to remember the New Testament directive from James: "You must understand this, my beloved: let everyone be quick to listen, slow to speak, slow to anger."[1]

One of us heard grumblings from a member of the congregation about the frequent use of illustrations from the civil rights movement and what the parishioner considered "Black issues." This complaint was common in a historically and still predominantly White congregation in the American South. Often, congregational objections seemed to stem from a deep discomfort with racial history, conflict, and even guilt. However, as the pastor chose to listen rather than jump to conclusions, and got to know the parishioner,

---

1. James 1:19.

they learned more about them. The parishioner shared that they were part of an unrecognized Indigenous group in the state. This particular Indigenous community had integrated quickly and largely peacefully with European colonists hundreds of years prior, leading to intermarriages and diverse descendants. As a consequence, the US federal government had never recognized them as a tribe with sovereign status. So, they were suffering not only the routine oppressions Indigenous peoples face but were also having their legitimacy as Indigenous people questioned. Their objections to focusing stories from the civil rights movement came from the pain of Indigenous oppression, and if the pastor had responded based on what they perceived as the normal stereotypes of White resistance to Black liberation, they would have missed a unique local pain that needed addressing. Indigenous experiences, then, made their way into sermon illustrations in the future, a balm on Sundays to Indigenous church members.

Consider some of these exercises you could use to enhance not only your own learning of your congregation but how they can learn more about themselves.

Activity to cultivate listening: Photos as a response

Have your congregants submit images focused on the church itself that represent where they see a need, where they have hope, and where they have fear. Print the photos and display them on storyboards or around the walls in a room. Depending on the size of the group, individuals can share their photos, or leave a written description (encourage them to be brief).

An example from a traditional but shrinking downtown church: One member took a photo of the nursery and described it as a place where they see the future of the church (hope). But then they submitted a different angle from the same room that provided a glimpse of the need for new toys and supplies (need). Lastly, they presented a third photo also from the nursery, which showed faded tags with children's names that had not been updated in years because the church had not had any new babies (fear).

PART II. Leading in Community

Activity to cultivate listening: Telephone game

Ask people to gather into diverse pairs. The first person in each pair (Allison) shares a "help" (I need help with . . .), a "thanks" (I am thankful for . . .), and an "awe" (I am in awe of . . .) about their life. Encourage the speakers to limit themselves to one-sentence answers. The second person in the pair (Brad) simply listens attentively and aims to remember what is said. Reverse the sharing: now Allison hears from Brad. Then direct the participants to each find a new partner and share with their new partner their previous partner's "thanks," "help," and "awe." Repeat the pair shuffle a few times, mixing pairs depending on the size of the group. Finally, in the end, have each person write down the name and answers of the final person they were repeating on a sticky note and stick it to the wall. Then invite everyone to find the sticky note about themselves and either correct or affirm the answers. Depending on the size of the group, either share aloud what was correct or false or allow the group to walk around and read what was on each sticky note.

> Questions to Consider
> In your listening, ask these questions of yourself based on what you learned from your congregation:
> Do their concerns align with yours and one another's?
> Do they enjoy the same things you do and as one another?
> If so, can you build experiences around awe together?
> Are there ways to incorporate their gratitude into specific celebration experiences?
> If not, is this an opportunity to share and teach?
> Do they share the same hopes and dreams for the church as you and one another do?
> If so, how might you put these hopes and dreams into action?
> If not, how might you discern together the dreams God has for your congregation?

NARRATING

Another important aspect of learning about your community is gaining an understanding of how the community functions as an organism individually and as a part of the larger whole. In other words, are they aware of the invisible web of connection to one another and their larger community? Ultimately, this is the art of storytelling and narrating. Oftentimes communities have unofficial bards or keepers of the communal stories. If you're fortunate enough to have one or more of these gems, ply them with food and drink, and settle yourself into an evening of listening, laughing, and learning. Appointed (or self-appointed) church historians, parliamentarians, and other granularly focused leaders in your congregation are often hubs for this kind of information. Another source could be hosting church-wide storytelling events, where we offer a microphone, some prompts, maybe some pointers and guidelines for what and how to share, and an attentive audience, and just see what emerges. It is important that these stories are shared with new members and that new members are allowed to reframe the story of the congregation. After all, as soon as the "we" becomes more than just me and you, but now me, you, and them, the "we" has changed. Collectively, *we* now share a new story formed from the old one.

Therefore, it is also necessary to evaluate when and whether the congregation is telling a realistic story about themselves. How do they think they are seen in the community versus how are they really seen? Who do they think they are versus who they have actually become?

One of the co-authors was called to serve as a resident pastor at a congregation that was thirty years old. In its beginnings, the church had been a plant of the big steeple downtown congregation that recognized the city was expanding to the west and land could be purchased cheaply for future growth of the congregation. They immediately built three structures in the middle of the four acres on this new property—an education wing, a chapel that seats 150, and a fellowship hall. Four years into the church plant, they were

Part II. Leading in Community

already hosting two worship services and had a membership roll of 500+. So they contracted with a developer for the next phase of their property.

Fast forward almost thirty years later to the arrival of their resident pastor, a thirty-three-year-old minister with no experience as a senior pastor, and now the only full-time staff. The music director volunteered his time to lead the six-member choir, and a very post-retirement-aged administrative assistant printed the bulletins and deposited the checks. Otherwise, all other duties of the church were carried out by the remnant of the congregation, now down to twenty-five.

In the first couple of weeks of the pastor's arrival, the congregants shared beautiful stories about their connections to the community, their history full of joys and triumphs, the calling they felt God had given them, and their hopes and dreams for the future. While they knew that a congregation that had shrunk from 500 to twenty-five in thirty years was not thriving, they did not describe themselves as dying.

Nothing could emphasize this disconnect between how they told their story and the true narrative of who they were more than the cover of their bulletin. For almost thirty years, week after week, the cover was a beautiful architectural drawing of the sanctuary they had planned to build but were never able to complete. And no one even batted an eye when the new pastor questioned how they still clung to this dream.

Three years later, as the resident pastor concluded his time with them, the congregation was finally able to see themselves and tell their authentic story. A year later, they donated their $4 million property to the Volunteers of America and began attending the original church that had planted them thirty years earlier, formally closing down the church plant. They celebrated who God had called them to be and who they now were.

Activity to cultivate story: Timeline of peaks and valleys

You may want access to the archives of newsletters and/or church minutes for this activity. Provide a long roll of butcher paper on the wall. In chronological order starting from the church's founding on the left to today on the right, note the name of significant events and include the year (event/date written at the bottom with a vertical line running to the top). The events could be times of change (pastor arrival/departure, new buildings, worship service changes), times of celebration (running two full services on Sunday morning, eighteen babies born in one year), or times of crisis (significant deaths, a fire). Events can also correlate to things happening in the city, state, nation, or world (tornado, downtown riot, pandemic). The people in the room decide what is significant to include.

Then, with sticky notes, individuals write a little more about what they can remember that may have been a response or action that happened within the congregation related to that date. Responses must be confined to one sticky note in length, and the author of the note should sign their name. Place the sticky notes up high on the paper if you think the response was a peak (we responded positively, helped, and grew closer together) and down low if you think the response was a valley (we responded in a way that caused harm, hurt, or divided us). Look at the peaks and valleys together and discern what stories can be told about who you are as a congregation and how your community may see you.

> Questions to Consider
> Consider these questions to ask yourself and, perhaps most importantly, your congregation in their narration:
> What stories do we choose to tell about our congregation? Why?
> What stories do we hide? Why?
> What might God be saying to us as a community? Where can we see God at work?
> Does our local community know our story? Would they tell the same stories about us?

Part II. Leading in Community
SCOPING OUT YOUR COMMUNITY

More anthropologist than tourist, your work in becoming a political pastor and engaging your church with your community at a deeper level will involve peering into both the sacred and unholy depths of your community with patience, care, and attention. You will invariably be challenged and changed by your encounters with others who speak, think, and live differently from you. It can be a steep learning curve, but we can say with confidence based on experience: it's worth it! We can also offer you some ideas to begin and sustain your journey. The very first step is to get to know your community in a deeper way than you have before.

Zoom Out

Step back and take a look at your community as a whole. This requires, first, that you define how much of the community you want to focus on. If you are in an urban area, perhaps you want to look at the five miles surrounding your congregation. If you are in a small town, you might want to look at the whole town. Start by drawing or printing a map. Notice how the community is constructed—the major roads, where business and industry are located, where schools, parks, libraries, and other community resources reside, and where people live. Focus on a general overview rather than getting too detailed at this point.

Think about the land, natural features, and wildlife in your community. How have they given shape to this place? Who are the major employers—historically and presently? Why do people come to this community? Why do they leave or stay? Notice the places your congregation frequents in your community and which ones they don't. Let yourself be curious. Generate a list of questions about "why" your community is the way it is. This is a time for big-picture wondering and wandering.

We also suggest looking at demographic data on your community, which you can find on city or county websites. This will help you get a clearer picture of the age, racial/ethnic makeup, and income level of people living in your community. Data sometimes challenges our assumptions about who our community is in helpful ways.

One of the ways we did this in our clergy cohorts was to provide a map of each pastor's geographic community and put it on the wall. Each pastor then explained their community based on the map, highlighting the big picture of their community, not just the individual activities of their churches. Some of them already had deep knowledge of their communities and others gained that knowledge over time.

When one cohort member was planting a church in Maine, the first thing their team did was to map their community. They called up area pastors and asked them a series of questions about their existing congregations and what they knew about the needs of the community. Then, they went to the websites of the US Census Bureau, the Pew Research Center, and the Barna Group. After that, they walked through different neighborhoods, played at the local playgrounds with their kids, and spoke with neighbors, the police department, and school teachers, asking questions about how their neighborhoods had changed over the years. What they found was remarkable.

The economy of the town had been built around a paper mill, and the mill had ground to a halt over the previous ten years, leaving the citizens of the town stranded in aging homes with tanking real estate value, rising poverty, and drug-related crime. Adding to that complexity was a seasonally swelling and shrinking college student population and a deep rift between the "college" and the "blue collar" sides of town. That rift had recently been exacerbated by a failed effort to merge the two shrinking elementary schools from each side of town.

The cohort member's church was located on an island in a river dotted with other islands. Nuns from the local Catholic chapel and moms they met at the playground both told them that all of the islands in the river had originally been promised to the Penobscot Nation. However, the founders of the local university, through deceptive means, had reappropriated the island for

Part II. Leading in Community

themselves. That was a deep wound in the community that had never been healed.

All of that information would have been hard for the cohort member to gather without talking to community members. It proved invaluable in helping them in understanding the community and discerning where God might be calling them to get involved.

Activity: WhatsApp Walk

One example of a way the pastor can get to know their community is by organizing what is sometimes called a "WhatsApp Walk." WhatsApp is a commonly used smartphone app that makes it easy to quickly share photos and text messages. But any group messaging function will work, and there are very low-tech possibilities as well. Find a group in your congregation or community that will commit to going for a walk in diverse pairs or small groups for an hour. They walk around the neighborhood or community, and every five minutes or so, the group leader can send a short prompt. "Post a photo of a sign of possibility." After a few minutes, "Post a photo of a scene that disappoints you." The prompts can be developed in service of what it is you want to learn about your community or from the congregants on the walk. These often turn playful and fun, building community among those who walk together and are almost always surprising in uncovering information about communities and fueling and identifying possibilities for community action.

As you continue in this process of looking at the big picture of your community, there are many helpful tools and resources, like asset mapping and power mapping (discussed in chapter 6: "Responding with Your Community") that you can draw upon to guide your learning.

Zoom In

Now that you've seen your community in broad strokes, you can zoom in on one or several aspects of your community. You may focus your inquiry on a particular geographical section of your community, on particular people, or on an area of concern, such as healthcare. There are many different lenses you can utilize depending on your goals.

As you move out into your community, we think it's enormously important that you pay attention to how you are cultivating relationships with people who have social locations different from yourself or your congregation. As a reminder, "an individual's social location is defined as the combination of factors including gender, race, social class, age, ability, religion, sexual orientation, and geographic location."[2] We imagine that you agree about the importance of diversity and listening to voices from multiple perspectives. What we want to acknowledge is that it takes effort, energy, and time, perhaps more than you feel like you have. So, you will need to be intentional about cultivating diverse relationships. Trust will need to be built. Humility will be required. You may experience multiple failures in connecting, so persistence will be necessary.

Activity: Listening sessions

One way you can foster these sorts of relationships and acquire this knowledge is through listening sessions. A strategy born out of community organizing, the listening session centers the community in diagnosing its strengths and challenges. A good listening session typically involves a group of ten or fewer (or multiple groups of this size in a large space) with one facilitator. The facilitator, which can be the pastor or another church leader, begins with a general prompt that can go something like this: What keeps you up at night? What makes you angry about living here? Where does

---

2. National Council on Family Relations, "Inclusion and Diversity Committee Report."

Part II. Leading in Community

it hurt? Allow respondents to speak about their experiences and designate one person in the group to take careful notes. In the end, take the responses from the group (or groups) and distill them into common themes. They may be housing, healthcare, education, or any number of things. You can either conclude by honoring their contributions or additionally ask them what they want to do about what they described. Community organizers often use this process to set their agendas so they reflect the wisdom and pain of the community in which they live and serve.

Again, we believe it's worth it. When you take time to listen and be present in these public spaces and take time to develop relationships with diverse community leaders, you are already becoming a pastor in the public square. You may even (and we think you likely will) begin to see the community as your parish. And we trust that this expanding horizon will enliven your ministry.

Go Backward

Listening to your community doesn't just involve the present circumstance. Another helpful way to learn about your community is to look back at its history. What major events or policy decisions have shaped it into the form it takes today? What stories give it color and contours? There are some obvious places to turn to in seeking answers—a local museum, for instance. You can often find a community archivist or a very knowledgeable librarian who can help. Most places have monuments in parks or government buildings that provide clues. And there are people in your community who remember or who have inherited the history of the place. But how exactly can the past inform you about the present? Consider this example:

One of the co-authors of this book is from Austin, a city that prides itself on being a progressive oasis in the heart of Texas. However, when you start looking into the history of Austin, a different story emerges. Interstate 35 bifurcates present-day Austin. West of the interstate is the University of Texas at Austin, the major business district, and affluent and mostly White neighborhoods. East of the interstate are historically African American and Mexican American neighborhoods where there is much less wealth (though gentrification is rapidly changing the makeup of these communities). Looking at Austin, you might assume it's always been this way, but it hasn't. At the beginning of the twentieth century, small communities of African Americans lived in neighborhoods throughout the city, many of which were historic Freedman communities. Everything changed in 1927 when the city adopted a new plan for the city's growth and development. The plan suggested that city officials work to remove African American Austinites from their neighborhoods west of East Avenue (now I-35) and segregate them in East Austin, the location of the city's slaughterhouse. It accomplished this by ending public services like water and trash collection to any African Americans living outside the designated zone. The city plan transformed the entire city of Austin; by the 1940s, almost all African Americans had relocated to East Austin. Furthermore, the City's Industrial Development Plan of 1957 zoned all property in East Austin as industrial, including single-family homes. This meant that the most polluting industries in the city were located and remained in this area. For instance, all the city's trash was hauled to and burned at an incinerator located in the heart of that community. Residents nearby said that ashes from the incinerator would rain down on their vegetable gardens. Due to these conditions and "this zoning, few residents were able to get bank loans (red-lining) for repairs or replacement of their original homes, leading to deterioration" of the housing stock, according to The Mayor's Task Force on Institutional Racism and Systemic Inequities Final Report.[3] Horrifically, a similar story is told in almost every major city across the United States.

---

3. The Mayor's Task Force on Institutional Racism and Systemic Inequities, "Final Report (2017)," 19.

Part II. Leading in Community

> Questions to Consider:
> You may want to pursue one or all of these specific questions as you explore your community's history:
> Who originally inhabited your land?
> Who settled in your community—when and why?
> Has there been any major in-migration or out-migration of people in the last half-century? What drove that?
> What policies have affected how people live and work (redlining, zoning, etc.)?
> Has any major event or tragedy changed your community?
> When you undertake this kind of historical exploration, you are looking for the ethos of your community, for the stories and policies that have shaped its pattern of common life.

Be curious about the stories your community tells about itself in the same way you are about your congregation. Some stories have taken center stage, while others have remained off to the side or hidden. How do you uncover the range of stories that exist? What stories do people further away from the centers of power and influence have to share? With all the different stories you encounter, you can ask: What or whom do they depict? What are they communicating and why? Who is telling the story, and who is left out of the story?

Pastors are well-positioned to hear stories. You tell stories and interpret stories as part of your ministerial role. You look for the ways in which God's story intersects with the lives of your congregational members. As a pastor in the community, you can consider how a story gives strength to your community and/or how it limits your community's imagination in detrimental ways. And you can help shape a more life-giving story, one that invites people into a broader vision of who they can be together.

As a method, consider using the peaks and valleys exercise named above with a group of community members, not just from your church.

Go Forward

You can learn about your community by listening to its longings and aspirations. What do people want for themselves and their loved ones? How can you help bring those hopes to fruition? The aim will be to develop your vision to notice where God is already at work in your community, stirring hearts or initiating action. Then, you will need to identify how you and your congregation can join alongside what God is already doing. The work of engaging your community will be discussed in the next chapter—once you have done some of the learning and listening that precipitates action. For now, you might consider yourself a spy for hope. What beautiful vision for a flourishing city can you discover and amplify as a pastor? How do you find it?

Visioning Activity: The World That Should Be

Gather a group of community members, ideally both people inside and outside your congregation. Draw an arrow on a board for everyone to see. On one side of the arrow, write "The world that is," and on the other side, write "The world that should be." Spend several minutes asking the group to articulate what the world looks like for them. What problems do they face? What things are not right? What's not working? Then, shift to the other side of the arrow. Have the group come up with counterparts to each thing they wrote under "the world that is" and describe what they think the world should be like. The exercise isn't about finding out how to get there (that's the arrow) but rather casting a vision of how they think the world should be.

Provoke their imaginations and you might be surprised at the wonderful vision of the future that already exists within your community.

Part II. Leading in Community

THE LESS YOU KNOW

In all of the ways of learning, the pastor positions themselves as a sort of clue collector. This metaphor can be useful for framing your experience. The pastor who focuses on clues looks upon the rocky soil or shallow soil, the thorns, and the predators upon the trodden paths. They look within the halls of the church, the shops on the street corner, and even in the halls of government for the competencies and curiosities of congregants and community members. Consider turning regular duties into clue collection. Your pastoral visits are not just for comforting people in sickness, visiting those who cannot leave their homes, and addressing prayer requests. Each visit can provide vital clues about your community and how well it's functioning (or not) for people. Clue-collecting into our hearts and minds is also a way to keep from over-functioning or rushing toward solutions. You will find that clues are everywhere but sometimes clues coalesce and call for an intentional response.

The more you collect clues, the more you become cognizant of the breadth and depth of your community and the invisible web that connects all. In that, you become increasingly aware of not just what you know but what you don't know. Humility about the world is crucial for the pastor as a political leader. But humility about oneself, as a character trait, is not quite what we mean here. The Renaissance cardinal Nicholas of Cusa spoke of a "learned ignorance" (*docta ignorantia*). By that, he meant a sustained discipline of wonder at the contradictions, paradoxes, and complex truths in the world. We might know *that* something is true without knowing *how* something is true. When consternation at a puzzling reality threatens to supplant curiosity, you can choose instead to adopt a posture of awe that leads you to want to know more. The learning process isn't something you do once at the beginning of your ministry career or when you start at a new place. Learning is continual and a discipline you never leave behind.

The steps of learning your community by zooming out, zooming in, going backward, and going forward are not meant to be seen as a linear process. This learning process is more labyrinthine,

Learning the Layers of Your Community

iterative, and dynamic. What you learn will be both ordinary and extraordinary. Expect surprise and expect disappointment. As you continue deeper into the heart of your community, we encourage you to make a habit of changing your focus and your perspective to keep seeing in fresh ways. It is also a more profound experience when you process it with a clergy community group. May your heart, mind, and soul continue to be enlivened in the process.

You may find yourself extremely energized as you learn and accumulate more and more knowledge of the history of your community and its present problems, or you may feel fatigued. Regardless, the next step requires the recognition that you can't do something about everything you've learned. You need another skill: discernment.

5

Discerning Where and How to Act

OUR COHORTS OF PASTORS examined a range of issues facing their congregations and communities. Where one group examined water rights because their region was already feeling the effects of water shortage, another group located in one of the fastest growing regions of the country looked at access to housing. The total list of issues addressed seemed a nearly comprehensive list of urgent areas for engagement: racism, prison, criminal justice, healthcare, migration, mental health, education, workplace issues, the arts, governmental relations, secularization, the environment, and more and more. On the one hand, the breadth was impressive and demonstrated the rich tapestry of work our pastors were helping to weave; on the other hand, the ever-growing list showed just how great the demands on the attention of the pastor as a political leader are today.

Most pastors work with few external forces governing or focusing their attention. They operate without much supervision and often without many opportunities for professional collaboration, which comes with advantages and disadvantages. A highly motivated, highly skilled pastor may not have to wait for middle management to sign the approval forms before beginning a new project or taking a new direction. A congregational council/session/vestry might say otherwise, but in most cases, pastors have a lot of latitude. At the same time, pastors who work without the benefit of a large staff or oversight need to carefully structure and use their time so that they align their attention with the exigencies of ministry. Sometimes, the freedom of autonomy gives you just enough latitude to get into trouble, be it by wasting time or chasing the wrong thing.

In discerning how to utilize your time, energy, and resources, we urge you to turn to those tried and true practices that help you listen for the movement of God's Spirit. Whether that be sitting in quiet contemplation, meditating on Scripture, or walking while praying through your community, the point is to build in intentional time to slow down and listen for clues about your next step or to gain a clearer sense of a guiding vision. The evangelical leader Charles Hummel wrote a pamphlet in the 1960s that became something of a sensation, titled *The Tyranny of the Urgent*. Not all of his solutions to the problem have withstood the test of time, but his initial insight still holds: unless a pastor has discerned a direction, gathered a series of partners, and articulated a vision, their time will most likely be taken up by the needs of those who seek the pastor out, even if given a thirty-hour work day.[1]

---

1. Hummel, *Tyranny of the Urgent*, 3.

Part II. Leading in Community

One of our colleagues is a compassionate listener who makes time for those who need her counsel, her help, or simply her attention. It would be so much easier and less time-consuming to say, "Here's a $20 gas card. Good luck." This kind of thing happens all the time. Perhaps only pastors realize how vital both relationships and direct assistance can be. Choosing where to invest limited resources and energy is a critical part of pastoral discernment. Unfortunately, others will need a pastor's attention equally as much but happen not to come to her office, or are not able to come to her office, or are not even able to articulate their need fully. Two hours spent with one person inevitably means that nothing happens for unknown others.

ACKNOWLEDGE COMPLEXITY

Prioritizing your time begins with understanding the interconnectivity and interdependence of social problems. No one suffers in isolation from external forces. If you were to somehow create a flow chart of the major social issues facing your community and draw lines of causes, effects, and implications, you would have a profoundly messy picture. Sometimes these connections can lead to a sense of wonder and awe, as though our communities were kind of elaborate Rube Goldberg machines that surprise us in their interrelations.

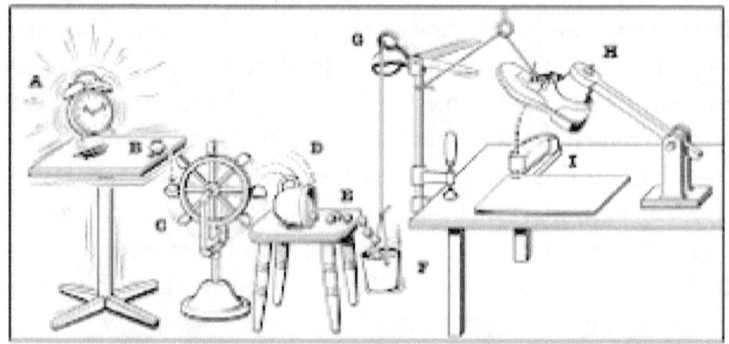

But more often, the complexities reinforce each other in ways that make it terribly difficult to match interventions with desired results. You see a loose thread and want to pluck it out, but when you do, not just the whole coat but the whole world seems to unravel with it.

We'll go over specific tools for analysis in the next chapter, as well as ways to address your findings, but for now, it's sufficient to say that we believe pastoral satisfaction flows in part from informed time management. The beginning of informed time management relies on an acknowledgment of the complex systems that make up our communities.

To get at this nested nature of social issues, consider the following two examples, one from a grand ecosystem and one from a small town.

Wolves

The reintroduction of wolves into Yellowstone National Park in 1995 had amazing but unanticipated consequences. Wolves were native to the ecosystem but had been driven away, killed off, and died out in the early part of the twentieth century. Some intrepid scientists proposed to reintroduce a small number, partly to help cull the exploding population of deer and elk. Overgrazing by these animals had drastically reduced the health and diversity of plant life in the park. But not even the wisest among scientists could have guessed the consequences of how far downstream the effects of the reintroduction would go. It became an example of something called a "trophic cascade" as a trickle of wolves led to a deluge of biodiversity.

First, the wolves did what they were expected to: they killed and ate a few deer and elk. But the shift in the food chain changed the behavior of the surviving deer. They bunched up together more for the sake of safety. They spent a bit less time in the grassy open areas by the Yellowstone River. They took cover farther up the slopes of the mountains. Immediately the places where they felt most vulnerable—the gorges with only one way in and out, for example—exploded with rich plant life.

Trees grew up as well. Rather than being devoured as saplings by grazing creatures, willows and aspens survived long enough to become brittle-barked and less preferred by the elk who had previously grazed them to the ground. More trees, and taller ones, meant immediately more songbirds and migratory birds made their home in Yellowstone. The levels of birdsong increased fivefold with surprising speed.

Critters that like trees even more than birds do are beavers. More beavers quickly moved to Yellowstone, and their housing projects gave shelter to muskrats and otters in due course, as well as more species of fish than those who can only live in a creek. Wolves don't eat mice, but coyotes do, so when wolves killed coyotes, more mice saw the light of day long enough to be snatched up by hawks.

The wolves were not themselves concerned with biodiversity, birdsong, or beavers, but their reintroduction had these effects. Similarly, the actions that we take in our communities lead to unintended consequences because every issue we address is connected to countless others. Additionally, we cannot handle every single problem that affects our community; however, with careful reflection and analysis, we can do the one thing that affects many others.

Shift Changes

As another example, one of the co-authors observed pastors in a small Midwestern community who were discussing, at a ministerium meeting, the fairly dramatic uptick in several kinds of social problems in the community. All had noticed increases in domestic abuse, divorce, and addiction troubling households and families. Each had different anecdotes but independently lacked a fuller understanding of the underlying causes. Nevertheless, it seemed anomalous, severe, and pressing to them. They devised a plan of trying to get to the bottom of it.

The pastors had conversations with their church members, and compared notes, consulted social service providers, law enforcement officials, and other entities that had some understanding of what was going on. These ministers came to a surprising conclusion that much of the stress in families was the disruption caused by sudden changes to the hours when workers were expected to begin and end their shifts. The ministers went back and asked earlier interviewees whether that had been a source of stress and disruption for their families. Time and time again, the answer was "Yes." It was surprising but made sense. Childcare is already difficult to come by, but how much more so when parents' work has constantly changing hours? Spouses saw less of each other and thus had more trouble communicating. Sleep patterns, household tasks, and so much else were disrupted. Shift changes were responsible for introducing the elements of chaos and dysfunction that, in turn, produced other social ills in the community.

The pastors asked for a meeting with the four largest employers in town and presented a united front asking for a change. The employers realized it was in their interest, as well as the community's, to make a change. A person with a terrible home life, who is about to be arrested on domestic assault charges, is losing their place to live, and is increasingly addicted to substances to cope with the pain, does not have a great list of traits for a job resumé. In response, the employers tripled the length of notice they gave any worker before their shift would be changed. Stress in families decreased dramatically.

In time, in Yellowstone, the cumulative impact of the migration of the elk and deer, as well as the return of the beavers, led to incredible change. The course of the river changed because of the reintroduction of the wolves. Likewise, addressing shift changes transformed household life, something pastors could otherwise have spent working on for years in small individual ways (like family counseling, childcare offerings, etc.). More than simply killing two birds with one stone, we can achieve transformation through careful and mindful attention to our communities and our own priorities. Wolves can change a river, and company paperwork

Part II. Leading in Community

can transform a family. Knowledge of what you're targeting and affecting in your community work will help you know how best to spend your time. Or, sometimes more importantly, how not to spend your time.

SLOW DOWN

The pastors who have participated in our leadership programs tended to be high achievers, perhaps uniquely vulnerable to this next challenge. Because many programs required a nomination for application, someone in a position of authority needed to have noticed the pastor's gifts and possibilities. This meant that there was a surplus of fast starters in the various cohorts. They were people who had quickly made their mark, solved a few problems, and even made a few headlines. There's a hidden danger there. The desire to act quickly and decisively is alluring because, for relatively simple problems, it works. Not so for the kinds of questions we're asking you to consider here.

In a southern city, a group of pastors gathered to attempt one of the community engagement strategies we'll discuss in the next chapter. All of these pastors were ambitious, talented, and driven clergy from a number of different traditions, and they were all people with different priorities. The group moved quickly to address what they saw as the central issues in their communities but their efforts fell apart. The pastors' network collapsed because they moved so quickly to issues and solutions without considering the slow, deliberate work necessary for tackling some of the most pervasive problems in the community. They skipped over some critical steps like listening to the community, building relationships with each other, and analyzing the structures and power dynamics of their communities. At any stage in their career, the driven pastor is vulnerable to moving too quickly and sabotaging themself. In this instance, it may take decades for another group of pastors to attempt a similar effort in this city and finally be successful.

Pastors will be more effective if they make room to listen deeply to others, particularly to those who have diverse viewpoints and life experiences. Approaching listening as a spiritual discipline, pastors listen to others as they "would listen to Scripture—attentively, mindfully and open to the Holy Spirit."[2] This practice of slowing down and listening prevents pastors from too quickly foreclosing on solutions to the problems they perceive. It may also bring new ideas to mind that they had not considered. Slowing down provides time for creative, multilayered responses to arise.

It is a generally accepted maxim in organizational theory that the more complex a system is, and the "higher up" in an organization chart one is acting, the less immediate the solutions can be. For example, a guidance counselor at a high school may have a dozen students seeking internships but only has time or resources to place six. Rather than not addressing the needs of the other six (and certainly not by placing them directly themself or demanding an increasingly frantic level of work from the guidance counselor), a principal may decide to appoint a part-time position whose responsibilities would include overseeing internships. That's one solution that will likely solve ten problems (even as it may add a couple of different ones).

Something like that is true in community-based ministry. There are times when quick and decisive action is called for, and effective pastors can swiftly act and do so with the confidence that their time is well spent. But when organizations get more complex (as all our communities do), and as problems become stickier, an effective pastor will often slow way down. Whatever methods of analysis they employ to test their initial hunches about how to act, they will take the time to make sure that their interventions aren't merely addressing surface-level symptoms.

Consider another example of this dynamic. A mostly White congregation in a racially diverse neighborhood decided to host a community event one Saturday per month. The event featured a professional hairdresser offering a free class for fathers, specifically, to bring daughters so they could learn how to braid their hair.

---

2. This language is adapted from Parker Palmer's "Touchstones" used in The Center for Courage and Renewal's Circles of Trust Retreats, https://couragerenewal.org/circle-of-trust-retreats/.

Fathers and daughters both enjoyed the event, but the impact went beyond enjoyment. There were many downstream results of this ministry that would have been hard to predict. Many of the fathers did not have custody of their children, but Saturday was a visit day for them. Being able to take their daughters to a special event felt good. Many of them struggled with relating to their daughters because they felt they had less in common than they did with their sons. Many were envious of the special relationships the girls had with their mothers. Being able to be the expert at a delicate and intricate hairstyle felt empowering and fun. What's more, there was more racial diversity at the church on Saturdays than there had been on Sundays. New friendships were formed.

SAY "NO" OR GIVE GENTLE ATTENTION

Discernment of your time and priorities requires not just slowness but also careful refusal of some work over other work. One of us describes this as giving gentle attention to issues we know we cannot fully commit to. Given the vast network of community and congregational relationships pastors need to maintain, a simple "no" is often insufficient. For that reason, pastors often wind up saying "yes" to things they had no business committing to because that's easier than a nuanced refusal. Pastors as political leaders, however, need to know how to validate others in their work and encourage long-term endeavors while not necessarily adding their own labor to the mix.

One of the authors noted the challenge of simply walking across the street. On the east side of the street was their congregation, and on the west side, a motel where the most marginalized lived on a daily or monthly basis. The street might as well have been a chasm, but the pastor was constantly asked what the church should do about it. She could have given the issue a large share of her attention, especially when she heard requests to do something about the motel. Instead, she decided to hold it gently.

One Easter, the church decided to hire a taco truck to provide food for the neighborhood. They decided to park the truck in the motel lot across from the church, and little by little, congregants crossed the street to eat tacos, drink coffee, and stand around awkwardly. The church repeated the event and, with each gathering, became more comfortable. Tacos were called for and delivered. One resident of the hotel tipped the cook because he wanted to "do his part because he enjoyed it." By the third gathering, one congregant paused after delivering a taco to the second floor. He sat down on the balcony with a motel resident of about the same age. The resident showed him a picture of his granddaughter, to which he said, "Hey, I am a grandfather too!" The men sat there swinging their legs off the balcony and talking as the Easter morning organ began to play. Because the pastor had the discernment to give the motel a gentler form of attention, an opportunity to create a beloved community with neighbors was realized.

WHEN TO EMPLOY PROPHETIC AND PASTORAL APPROACHES

Discernment is critical for the pastor as a political leader, not just in setting your priorities but in the posture you take toward them. Sometimes you need to push for something aggressively, while a gentler touch may be necessary in other situations. You may need to raise the temperature in the room one day, and you may need to work to lower it and be a non-anxious presence the next. In a time of apathy or even outright resistance, you might need to drive a congregation or community in a new direction. However, in a time of exhaustion or trauma, you may need to step back and simply listen, care, and comfort. A simple, yet still instructive, way to characterize these differing stances would be what many have referred to as the prophetic or the pastoral.

The prophetic response is like when God says through Isaiah, "Your new moons and appointed festivals my soul hates; they have become a burden to me; I am weary of bearing them." And, "Cease to do evil; learn to do good; seek justice; rescue the oppressed."[3]

---

3. Isaiah 1:14; 16–17.

Part II. Leading in Community

The pastor, as a political leader in the prophetic stance, demands change and justice when things aren't right. This posture is often coupled with public proclamation and public action.

One of us was accompanying a church member to their usual check-in with Immigration and Customs Enforcement (ICE) when the church member was abducted and taken into custody. The pastors at the church and the congregation rallied behind their detained church member, making the public aware of the injustices he was suffering in his ensuing incarceration and the dangers he faced if deported. For forty-five days, the entire congregation, led by its pastors, fought against the impending removal by engaging with representatives (who discussed the situation in the House of Representatives), senators (who tried to help them navigate bureaucratic channels in Washington), and even ICE itself with legal assistance, parole filings, and public pressure. After those forty-five days, their church member was still deported, but their town has never forgotten the prophetic leadership the church and its pastors put on display. The church now sits at the center of confronting numerous justice-related concerns in its community.

The pastoral response is like when God urges Isaiah, "Comfort, O comfort my people, says your God. Speak tenderly to Jerusalem, and cry to her that she has served her term."[4] In many cases, you cannot push someone dealing with great pain or weariness to do or be more. At that moment, what they need is their pastor, even in the capacity of a political leader, to comfort them in their affliction. This posture is necessary both inside and outside the traditional congregational community. When the whole community is faced with a crisis, sometimes the pastor's role is to tend to the suffering caused by the crisis before moving directly to a solution.

A pastor from one of the cohorts in inner-city Baltimore, Maryland, described the challenge of discerning whether he was called to a prophetic or pastoral response when leading his church to respond to emerging needs during the early days of the COVID-19 pandemic. With little public transportation and only gas stations and small convenience stores open, his neighborhood

---

4. Isaiah 40:1–2a.

lacked access to basic supplies like hand sanitizer, face masks, and gloves. When those supplies did arrive, they were often sold at a 50 percent markup. The pastor tried to spur his congregation into action. He pushed his denominational synod for funds and supplies. He drove hundreds of miles, sometimes daily, to pick up items from friends, other churches, and nonprofit organizations. He did the lion's share of the work. Eventually, the pastor realized that the congregants themselves, mostly elderly and medically fragile, did not have the capacity to care for the community. They were frightened, depressed, isolated, and anxious. Even when told what they could do, they were incapable in that moment of responding. Before approaching the necessary solution, the pastor realized his community needed care.

The prophetic and pastoral approaches are not mutually exclusive. The effective pastor as a political leader must employ both. Discernment between the two is a skill you only learn over time and in community with other pastors, and it requires a degree of trial and error and some measure of getting it wrong. It's important to continue learning when to lean on which approach so that you don't lock yourself into one mode of ministry. A pastor who privileges the pastoral approach can find themselves ineffectual in the face of conflict. Likewise, the pastor who privileges the prophetic approach can find themselves inadequate in the face of pain.

Once you have discerned your issues and your posture toward them, you need a mode of response, the subject of our next chapter.

6

Responding with Your Community

WHEN YOU MOVE INTO a new community, inevitably you confront a crisis of unfamiliarity. The ways people speak, act, and relate to one another are different from one community to the next. Similarly, when you consider the role of pastor as political leader in a new way, the newness of it all can be overwhelming. In this book, we are encouraging you toward some new pathways you may not have considered but which we believe are transformative for you, your congregation, and hopefully your community. The lessons many of our cohorts draw upon come from sources we never encountered in educational training or any ministerial environment. They come instead from our intersections with other vocations, traditions, and work. Whether you are just starting a new position or a new career, or maybe you're at a frustrating or listless midpoint in either, we hope to show you new ways to look at your community and respond within it. Road construction in a community where you have lived for a long time, for example, can cause you to drive a different way, notice different things, and ask different questions. So too can considering novel ways of responding to your community.

PREPARING A THOUGHTFUL RESPONSE

Many pastors as political leaders respond to their communities as solo actors to immediately address issues of need or crisis. Rather than flying solo into a strong headwind of need, there are far more effective strategies for community engagement. And before engaging the community and its challenges, a pastor can benefit from doing some of the infrastructure or backstage work that allows for a strong performance for the community. One of the great strengths of the pastoral leader is the power to convene and interpret. In these upcoming sections, we offer not only methods for community engagement but also encourage pastors toward the preliminary work of convening and interpreting that we believe will fuel stamina and vitality in the vocation of ministry.

Before rushing toward solutions or even methods, consider the relationships and the community clues that will inform your meaningful public work. *How* you engage the clues and intersect with other community professionals will empower community analysis and contribute to the transformational possibilities that live deep within the heart of each pastor.

So, consider the groundwork necessary for each of these approaches. The following is not an exhaustive list, but those we found most valuable. Each one is different and has extraordinary value for the pastor, but each of them is distinct. Each community engagement method has drawbacks, but clues and competent leaders around you will help you discern a way forward when engaging your community. Perhaps one method would work best in one community or on some issue. A combination of methods might be what is called for when developing the most effective strategy. Training in and practicing each of them is a helpful addition to your toolkit for ministry. Conversations with your clergy peer may help you determine when to use the right method, particularly if your peer group includes diverse perspectives. More than just choosing a method based on the outcome, theological reflection in your cohort can help make the decision, as well. Each of these methods has different roles for stakeholders, decision-makers, power, and the pastor. Where the Spirit leads, you require careful discernment of the roles people and power need to play in a single moment in time. Your cohort can help you make those distinctions based on their diversity of experiences, theological perspectives, and individual commitments.

METHODS OF COMMUNITY ENGAGEMENT

The Needs-Based Approach

The needs-based approach does not often go by that name; in fact, it's something of a straw man for the other approaches as they attempt to distinguish themselves from other modes of problem-solving and community engagement. Nevertheless, what we might refer to as a needs-based approach is pervasive in attempts to remedy community problems, especially in churches.

The process of a needs-based approach usually goes something like this: Identify a problem in a community, research the problem, propose a solution, enact the solution, and then evaluate its efficacy. A government program, for instance, might be funded by legislation that seeks to address a problem. Once the legislation is passed, funding is secured, staff are assigned or hired, and the team engages in typical research processes to give themselves an adequate grasp of the issue at hand. They may engage other experts or be experts themselves, but the result of this stage may be a white paper, a proposal or plan, or some other prescription. The follow-through on that solution may come from the team or be executed by an external entity like a local government or nonprofit grantee (even a church!).

One of the authors of this book works at a church with a popular needs-based ministry. The Backpack Buddies program identified the needs of food-insecure households in one neighborhood. Children that received free and reduced breakfast and lunch got the great benefit of food while they were at school, but on the weekends, food sources were more limited. The church, in collaboration with the social workers at the neighborhood schools, started to put together "backpacks" of food to go home with kids on the weekends. They received a variety of foods, from snacks to quick, shelf-stable meals, in order to make it through the weekend without suffering from hunger. The program has been running for several years, providing weekend meals for well over a hundred families a week.

Any finger-wagger who would criticize a program that helps feed hungry kids is a fool. But if you do dig a little deeper, some real limitations appear. The analysis of the community for needs-based solutions usually comes from outside the community in regimented or unstructured ways. In the case of social services, there is often academic analysis of data that guides the implementation of programs and their funding priorities. In the case of the Backpack Buddies, the data is an observed need on behalf of the congregation. That may be the personal experience of a church member or the gradual observation of the pastor. In either case, it's a summary look at a community from without that provokes the solution.

You can get creative about the source of that analysis in your own work. One of our colleagues lives in a state with a nonurgent emergency number, the kind you might call if your electricity were about to be disconnected or if you feared but had not yet experienced impending domestic abuse. The records of that line can be shared and examined, which the pastor did with leadership in his

Part II. Leading in Community

congregation. They got to see a minute-by-minute account of the expressed needs in their community. There are many other ways. Consider shadowing another person who does community work. Follow a teacher for a day in your local public school. Ride along with a postal worker or first responder and learn about how they see your community.

The distinctiveness of this approach is its starting point and its relationship to the community. The journey begins with a problem in the needs-based approach. Who identifies that need may come from a variety of sources: the community itself, a committee, a legislator, a nonprofit leader, or a church group. The goal of the process is to solve that problem or meet that need. While the details may involve getting in the weeds, the process is generally pretty simple. See a need, meet a need.

But when you begin with the identification of need, you're starting with the point of deficiency in a community. Communities characterized only or even repeatedly by their deficiencies and needs are weakened in the long run. They understandably tire of being regarded from the outside as "those people who get our pity." Despite the good intentions of the helpers, the dignity of those helped is ignored.

Needs-based solutions also often struggle with sustainability. When addressing a need, you can find yourself filling a gap that never goes away. If a neighborhood lacks sources of food, for example, the continual operation of a church food pantry doesn't solve the problem that there's no grocery store with affordable produce. Until there is a change in the system, the needs-based solution will be perpetually necessary. That puts the individuals served at the mercy of fundraisers, lawmakers, and others with no proximity to the affected members of the community. What happens when those who hold the purse strings decide the needs-based solution is too expensive or that the problem isn't worth addressing? The program then dies, leaving the same problem it sought to solve in the first place. A single focus on needs-based work shows its limitations in the resulting pain.

An additional limitation of the needs-based approach is the role of stakeholders and decision-makers. In the needs-based approach, these groups rarely overlap, and they may not even be conversation partners at any point in the process. Usually, the decision-makers hold some position of power and have little direct accountability to the people who are going to be served by the solution. When the United States started its 2003 war in Iraq, just one of the 538 members of the House and Senate had a child serving in the military, even though many hundreds of them had adult children of an appropriate age. How might the decision-making have been different if there had been more politicians with a direct stake? Or to return to the church food pantry example, a wealthier church may run the program but see very few of its members use the service. The final decision-maker, whether it be a pastor, vestry, session, deacon, or trustee, has a degree of insulation from the actual need and the people experiencing that need. That can lead to erroneous or uninformed decisions. One pantry decided to change its practice of having clients fill their bags at the pantry rather than pick up an already-filled bag. The pre-filled bag is more efficient and may be more nutritious, but the decision-makers hadn't considered how much more dignity a client has in choosing their own food.

For all its potential faults, however, sometimes a needs-based approach is necessary. Disaster ministries, for example, often have to move swiftly to meet specific needs in the wake of a particular event. Sometimes people just need a roof over their heads and food in their stomachs as fast as they can manage it. Occasionally people do just need gas money. Likewise, sometimes community ills have been neglected for so long that a sort of ministerial triage is necessary simply to stabilize a problem before it can be addressed more sustainably. Churches should not close all their food pantries because they realize that needs-based approaches have some problems. Each of these strategies for community engagement has flaws. Expect some failure and mistakes.

One of the authors had an unsettling Sunday morning experience over the span of three Sundays. From the pulpit, on week one, the preacher could see through a narthex window a group of adults huddled and chatting in the back of the narthex. On week two, the pastor did not notice but the ushers noticed and reported to the pastor that about six people never came in for worship and talked with one another for the entire worship service. On week three, it happened again, and afterward, the pastor checked in with one of those adults gathered. In their conversation, it was revealed that the adults were gathering because they were all educators at a local elementary school. The school had recently doubled down on a policy for white sack lunches. The white sack lunch was the lunch a child received when their parents failed to pay on their lunch account. It included an apple, white milk, and a peanut butter and jelly sandwich. The teachers were concerned about the students' disappointment and lack of morale after lunch. They were huddled in the back of the narthex to strategize healthy and fun snacks for children so that they might recover from the white sack experience. This catalyzed the board of deacons to call for a meeting with the superintendent of the district. The church offered to pay the lunch bill for any child who was due to receive a white sack lunch. The school did not receive the gift but adjusted the policy for the well-being of the children. The novelty of this response may be found in the congregation's attention to the peripheral action/behavior at work in the life of the church as an essential clue revealing needs in the community.

The Asset-Based Approach

Asset-based community development emerged as an attempt to start from a different place than the classic needs-based approach. Instead of identifying a problem in a community, asset-based community development begins with what resources the community already has and how those assets can be used to further the well-being of the community.

The centrality of community members is critical to asset-based development. This approach recognizes explicitly that everyone has gifts, capacity, and interests in your community.

Rather than prescribe what must be done, asset-based community development asks, what is already here? People, rather than just programs, are at the center of this strategy. What can neighbors offer one another that would help both parties and the community as a whole thrive?

One of our author-pastors was in a burgeoning church community with extremely limited financial resources. Most of the church members were young families with small children, often struggling to make ends meet, but they had a desire to have an impact on their community. As they prayed and assessed what assets they each had to bring to the table, they realized that they each had a home to welcome other people into and a family to share. The local university, as it turned out, had a very large number of students from overseas who were not able to return home during holidays due to the cost of travel or visa complications. The students also expressed significant loneliness, as well as a great interest in learning about some culture and traditions of the US. So the church members began inviting the stranded and lonely students to their houses to share in their own family feasting and celebrations. They took students Christmas caroling, shared food from each other's traditions, played soccer in the yard, swapped stories about home life, culture, and hopes for the future. One particularly memorable student from Iran ended up getting married while finishing his degree, and the church family he had built a relationship with over the past several years stood in as a surrogate family at the ceremony when his own family was unable to attend in person. The church became a hub for overseas students to find a sense of home and belonging throughout their years away from their countries and families, and didn't need any more resources than an extra chair at their dining room tables.

With this focus on the individual and their relationships in a community, asset-based approaches require a great deal of listening. Rushing to action preempts the important time for active listening and reflection. Surprising solutions can emerge even from a quagmire of apparently unconnected issues.

Part II. Leading in Community

Consider the state of many mainline Protestant congregations in the United States: They have aging congregations and buildings and shrinking finances. Frequently, these congregations (you may be a pastor for one!) see their building as a liability and struggle to address their long-term sustainability (beyond cutting the pastor's salary, unfortunately). The property becomes an ill-fated albatross that sucks the life and potential out of the congregation. An asset-based approach might ask, what would it look like if we considered the building and property we have to be an asset to the community? How could what we already have assist with the thriving and well-being of ourselves and our neighbors?

Many churches in recent years have discovered that their properties are assets that address the crisis in affordable housing or the lack of noncommercial gathering space. If your church has a large education building that it no longer uses, how could that asset be transformed into a place for people to live? If your church has a fellowship hall that rarely sees non-Sunday gatherings, listening intently to the community might help the community see a space that could be used for everything from hosting recovery groups to an affordable quinceañera venue to being a community kitchen for those who want to can and preserve their own foods.

One of our churches realized that its building was far larger than it needed to be for the size of the congregation the church maintained. A full third of the building had fallen into disrepair from neglect and age. Rather than serving as a center for ministry, the building was storage for every knick-knack the church had accumulated for sixty years. Instead of looking at the structure as a liability, the pastor led the congregation to consider it as an asset. The property was right next to two public transportation stops, a pharmacy, a grocery store, and dozens of local businesses. It was the perfect location for affordable housing. Now, the congregation is in the process of repurposing half its land to meet a dire need in its community with what it had once considered to be its most serious liability.

Assessment of your community assets can bring surprising results. One of the most common methods is "asset mapping."

Asset mapping involves either looking at a neighborhood map or walking around the neighborhood to identify the community's assets. These may be businesses, nonprofits, transportation routes, or even individuals. You want to identify the capacities and abilities of your community, which is where the asset map can move beyond the literal cartography. Describe what the constituent parts of your community are capable of doing. Once you've been as exhaustive as you can be, step back and look at it. What could be done with all these assets? What is your community capable of? Answers may seem obvious from this approach that would have surprised you before undertaking it.

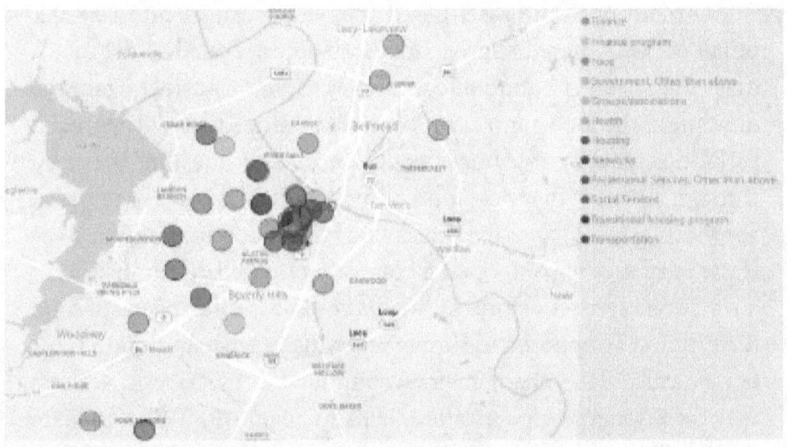

Asset Map of Waco, Texas by the Baylor School of Social Work in Collaboration with First Presbyterian Church of Waco. Michaela McElroy, Project Manager, used with permission by Dr. Gaynor Yancey of Baylor University's Garland School of Social Work.

The asset-based approach has sustainability among its chief advantages. When outside forces aren't determining the need and solution, community members have control of the process. Local control and the reliance on an interdependent web of relationships make it much more difficult for an initiative to fall apart. If funding for a local nutrition program is only sourced from the federal

Part II. Leading in Community

government, for example, the program can survive only to die based on an election or the opinions of a departmental secretary hundreds of miles from your community. Using local assets can circumvent those challenges to longevity.

Additionally, with an asset-based approach, there is often far more overlap between stakeholders and decision-makers. When an internal asset is being repurposed or brought to the wider community, the decision-makers controlling its use tend to be local and even count themselves among those who would benefit from the asset. There's typically no need for legislation, external funds, or anything else that would otherwise hamper the classic needs-based model.

At the same time, asset-based approaches can fall into a similar pitfall of needs-based approaches. Both approaches do little to address the systemic nature of community issues. Consider again the example of the food pantry. We know that the needs-based approach to food insecurity or hunger could be directly meeting the need through a pantry that puts food on people's tables. An assets-based approach might look at the skills of neighborhood residents and see if the resources exist to open a community-based co-op instead of a traditional grocery store. Residents could own the means of food distribution as opposed to simply receiving it. Such a solution is often radical and life-changing for a community, but it doesn't address why there wasn't a grocery store there, to begin with. What policies created the patterns of disinvestment that produced that food desert? Who has the power to change those structures?

No worthy cause is without its faults, and no single model of community engagement is perfect in every situation. But the perfect cannot be the enemy of the good.

One of the authors used the Sunday school hour to bring in community leaders to speak about their vocations and work. One local housing nonprofit CEO confessed in his time with the congregation the challenge there was to secure lots of land for home construction. Among those gathered, one person knew someone at the city level and made an email introduction between the nonprofit CEO and a recently retired city planner. That retiree took the ball and set up a meeting with relevant individuals in city government. At the meeting, everyone came to a greater understanding of the challenges, and the CEO had a much-needed network to secure land in a highly competitive market. Assets recognizing assets.

Community Organizing

Like the previous approaches, community organizing presumes a different starting point, which serves as a significant distinction. Community organizing sees the journey begin not with needs or assets but with relationships. Community organizing has as its center the "garment of destiny" of which we are all a part, to borrow a phrase from Martin Luther King Jr.[1] The relationships we have with one another drive change and shape our neighborhoods, communities, and societies. Harnessing the power of those relationships is the key to enduring change.

One way of understanding the realm of human relationships through community organizing is by dividing society into three spheres of influence. There's the government sphere, which includes everything from social programs to politicians and the bureaucrats between them. This sphere has the power of law and compulsion. There's the commercial sphere, which includes businesses, chambers of commerce, and other similar monied interests. The third sphere is the civic sphere, which includes working people and their associations (e.g., houses of worship, Lions Clubs, Rotary, etc.). The pastor is a leader within the civic sphere.

Each of these spheres is full of people with relationships to and with one another, and the spheres themselves interact. The dominant form of interaction between spheres today includes:

The civic sphere purchases goods from the commercial sphere and has limited influence via their wallets.

The government sphere is partially elected by the civic sphere and has limited accountability through the democratic process.

---

1. King Jr., "Letter from a Birmingham Jail," 75.

Part II. Leading in Community

The commercial sphere influences the government sphere through lobbying, funding campaigns, and other lucrative connections.

Power is used in these relationships through two primary means: organized people and organized money. The commercial sphere has an exceptional amount of organized money and is usually the most powerful actor putting pressure on the government sphere. However, there is often untapped power in the civic sphere through organized people. Community organizing seeks to harness that power for the common good.

Like asset-based community development, community organizing relies on significant overlap between the stakeholders and the decision-makers in its processes. Unlike needs-based and assets-based approaches, community organizing doesn't start with a concept or an issue. Instead, it focuses on building relationships in the civic sphere until there are enough organized people that can exercise power in negotiation with the government and commercial spheres.

The cycle of community organizing works like this: (1) relationship-building, (2) listening, (3) researching, (4) acting, (5) reflecting. After building relationships, community organizing involves listening to the broad base of your community to understand better what pressures they are facing. Once a pressure is identified, considerable time is spent by the community researching the pressure and potential solutions. Once a solution is identified, the community organizing group takes it to those who have the power to make it a reality and negotiate its enactment. Afterward, they reflect on the solution and the process before starting the cycle over.

A useful tool in community organizing is called "power mapping," which you can do with your congregation, your entire municipality, or any organized structure in between. A power map is the real organizational chart for your institution or community. While there may be an explicit chart of hierarchies and positions, communities often function on a less official structure. For example, in your church, you may have a committee structure for decision-making, but there may be some elders or respected members of the congregation who have the power to get things done. It can be helpful in your public life as a pastor to do some deliberate work figuring out what power structures are effective both in your church and the community around you. If you want to get something done, you need to know who has the power to accomplish it.

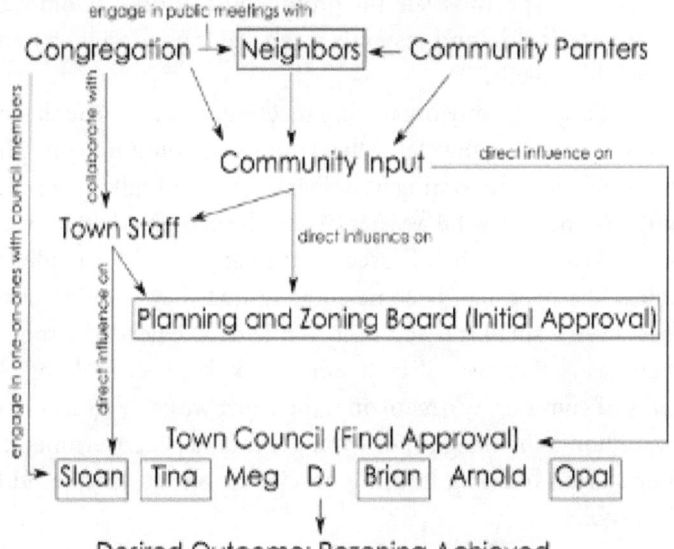

This approach has some advantages, including local ownership and sustainability. The virtue of subsidiarity is strong in community organizing efforts because there's not any outside influence on the prioritization of issues. While the researchers may consult experts (and should!), the researchers are community members who have direct experience of the issue at stake. The process also develops community leaders over time, people who are pastors, residents, workers, and others who have an express self-interest in sustaining the effort. The centrality of relationship-building also engenders an enduring character to the work so that it doesn't dissipate if one leader or institution pulls back or departs.

The limitations of community organizing derive from its strengths. The focus on relationship-building, leadership development, and researched local solutions makes it a very slow and methodical process. One of us involved in founding a broad-based community organizing effort spent four years building relationships between community leaders before ever moving to discuss a specific issue the group could address. Community organizing is slow and systemic work and is not designed to meet immediate needs.

At a community organizing meeting, a pastor articulated the frustrating feeling they felt when addressing community needs. So many people were coming into their church and calling the church office asking for rental assistance and the church could only do so much. Where the church used to put people up in extended-stay hotels, the need had become so great that they couldn't hope to meet even a small fraction of it. While people needed a roof over their heads, there was also systemic work that needed doing. After years of community organizing, the effort was able to secure over $9 million in housing funds from the municipal government, and they started building housing on church-owned land to address the problem.

It was wonderful work that will benefit the future residents of the housing built, but sadly it did little for those who needed a home *right then*. A needs-based solution is the only way they could have been helped at that time, but it required power the church didn't possess.

Advocacy

While some approaches hit problems directly and others seek to adjust the systems that create them, advocacy exists to influence the climate in which decision-makers address problems. If you've ever experienced an awareness campaign, signed a petition, marched in a protest, or spoken to your legislator about a problem as part of a group, you've been a part of advocacy work. As an approach to pastoral leadership, this one may be the most intuitive to those drawn to preaching and public proclamation as pastoral responsibilities.

Advocacy, like a needs-based approach, usually begins with a problem. How that problem is identified varies widely depending on the organization or leader doing the advocacy. Sometimes advocacy comes from an existing organization seeking its own interests in the legislature. Many nonprofits have "Advocacy Days," where they take their supporters to state capitals or Washington, DC to advocate for their cause. At other times, advocacy can be more homegrown, as we saw with the students from Marjory Stoneman Douglas High School advocating for gun laws after the horrific shooting. Usually, advocacy is a bit of a mix of both.

The purpose of advocacy is to shift the conversation about an issue with the hopes of achieving certain policy objectives. Advocacy for the pastor might look like hosting a letter-writing day with the congregation where they communicate with their elected representatives about an issue the congregation cares about. The pastor might convene clergy across their community to sign a petition urging a particular action. One of our colleagues' congregations regularly joins in writing letters to their representatives about issues the church cares about. They gather together at the church and mail their materials together to the appropriate parties. They've even received personal responses. One of us was once told by a politician that when they look at a room or receive a campaign of letters, they look at each person involved as potentially at least ten voters. Concerted advocacy efforts can therefore have a significant effect on how a politician views the climate around a particular issue.

Advocacy as a community engagement effort has the particular advantage that it does perhaps more for the participant than the target. Like the liturgical work of worship, advocacy work can transform the individual participant. It can reorient them to understanding or prioritizing an issue in a new way. Insofar as advocacy work raises awareness, it also adjusts the climate in which issues are discussed both inside and outside of your congregation. If housing has been a subject of intense advocacy work in your congregation, for example, that can shift the climate of your community when it comes to voting for rezonings, housing bonds, and other investments that might have otherwise failed in the past.

Advocacy, like the other approaches, also has its limitations. Advocacy does not meet the immediate needs of those enduring hardship. When you tell a legislator to put more public funds toward feeding programs, it doesn't immediately put food on the table for a food-insecure family that came into your office looking for help. Advocacy is also highly susceptible to outside influences as the largest advocacy organizations have their own elaborate bureaucracies and interests beyond the issues they want to solve. The work also comes with the temptation to see the social media post, petition, or protest march as the end result, the climax of the work. Participation can be gratifying in itself and cause us to forget the end goal.

A congregant in a local church called her pastor to report that her adopted son had sexually assaulted his sister. After this was reported to her, her son confessed. Both were minors. The mother, heartbroken, called the police and began due process according to the law. The pastor asked, "What can we do to help you?" The mother quickly and confidently replied, "You can talk about this and make sure our congregation knows what happened. Shed the light of day on it as you ask for prayers." The pastor did just that. In the announcements on Sunday, morning prayers were called for as the sexual assault was reported and due process had begun. The congregation responded as advocates in various ways. Two congregants wrote a letter to the district attorney indicating that the congregation did not hope for special treatment for this child of the church, but the church would stand by this young man through the due process. Several congregants organized letter writing over several weeks time as the boy transitioned. At the end of the transition period, as the boy took up residence in a rehab facility with a lot of boys much older than himself, one household wrote a weekly letter that included a joke and encouragement. The pastor wrote weekly as well. Other congregants found ways to talk about and process the situation, some dealing with their own trauma. Others did their part to reach out to support the mom and remaining children with encouragement as they sought counseling to process the ongoing experience. The congregation did their best in advocacy, providing updates in the bulletin and eventually welcoming the young man back at the end of the year of rehab.

COLLABORATION

We do not advise engaging in any of these strategies alone, either within your congregation or as a solo institution. All of them are best practices in collaboration with other leaders and institutions and in reflection with your clergy peer group.

Needs-based solutions can go further when we pool our resources. In one of our towns, churches came together to establish a shared ministry to meet material needs rather than simply running small, individual benevolence funds. At first, the larger food pantry served more people, but eventually, the ministry expanded into a multifaceted institution. Currently, it runs a thrift store, a food pantry, adult learning classes, and a whole host of social services. For better or worse, the organization was so successful that its coverage area was the last to receive a health and human services center in the county because the existing work being done was so promising.

Asset-based community development likewise shouldn't happen in a silo. The very act of asset mapping presupposes collaboration between community assets. You or your congregation may also not be aware of the full constellation of resources available in your community. What you could learn from other institutions may even vastly overshadow the collective knowledge within your congregation, great though it may be.

Community organizing is definitionally not done alone. Because it is dependent on relationships, no community organization exists in isolation. The broad-based community organizing

Part II. Leading in Community

group one of us helped start counts well over forty institutions as members, with its immediate reach numbering in the thousands, with more than a hundred trained leaders. Clergy and laity alike serve in critical research and leadership roles to achieve the aims of the organization, which are determined by listening sessions that depend on the input of thousands of community members, especially emphasizing diverse perspectives.

Advocacy, too, works best in partnership, not just with local organizations but even with national ones that have tested strategies and results. One letter to the mayor may not mean much, but 150 will cause them to pay some attention.

As a political leader, one of the pastor's greatest powers is the convening of allies in our struggles. None of us are called to go it alone. You are part of an invisible web of connectedness and mutuality, and it is helpful to see where you can turn for support. If any of these strategies intimidate you, know that you don't do them by yourself! As Paul reminded the Corinthian church, "You are the body of Christ and individually members of it," but each member of the body has a different and necessary function.[2] In convening all the parts of the body in the church, pastors bring together a wide array of gifts and experiences to help inform the solutions they might pursue. The same is true in the powers to convene community leaders and even to convene your pastoral cohort. The diversity of experiences, identities, and gifts in the congregation, cohort, and community all add essential components to your community work. Without them, these strategies will be far weaker and less enduring in their effects.

To do any of this work, however, we need to do one more thing: reflect.

---

2. 1 Corinthians 12:27.

7

Reflecting on Your Power

Reflecting

EVERYONE FROM ORGANIZATIONAL THEORISTS to on-the-ground community organizers typically agree that action should not be taken without reflection. Taking continuous action without pausing to reflect on the impact of those actions can lead both to being ineffectual and causing unintended harm. Instead, the pastor as a political leader needs to be able to contemplate their role in the community, particularly in the safe harbor of a clergy cohort. That requires considerable time thinking about a concept that has lingered in the background of previous chapters: the pastor's power.[1]

In some ways, it would be nice if, having come to a fuller understanding of the community's needs and assets, convinced of the course of action needed to bring about a longed-for change, pastors could simply snap their fingers and—presto change-o—make it happen. That would be efficient and immediate. But the opposite of efficiency . . . is love. Efficiency dispenses with empty spaces, pregnant pauses, and potentially redundant collaborations. In waving a magic wand to effect the change we want to see, we wave goodbye to the friendships and surprises that mark an admittedly messier but far more *loving* way of doing ministry. Pastors need to approach leading change in the community from a stance of love. But what exactly does that mean, and how does that work?

POWER, PER SE

We have to begin by considering the nature of power itself. If a family decides where they want to go on vacation but fails to consider how they will get there, they have a vision of an end but lack the means to achieve it. They haven't used the power available to them to get where they want to go. Likewise, if a committee decides on a course of action but ignores who will do what is needed to make it happen, they have not done meaningful work at all. There is a reason why Paul, when speaking to the notoriously conflict-ridden Corinthian church, says, "The Kingdom of God depends not on talk but on power."[2]

At a fundamental level, power is radically simple, neutral, and obvious. It is simple because it is the capacity to effect change. It is neutral because it can manifest in great, good, mediocre, bad, and

---

1. The pastor's power here should be distinguished from the term "transformative power" that we've used throughout this book. Pastors experience transformational power from engaging the multiple layers of community around them. When pastors experience transformation, it eventually gets shared as "pastoral power" through political leadership in the community.

2. 1 Corinthians 4:20.

evil ways. Power itself is simple, but our relationship with power is incredibly complex. That relationship is neither simple, neutral, nor obvious.

People are wary of power for good reason. Some forms of power have been horrific. Tyrannical regimes have used their power to perpetrate genocide, purges, and invasions. Reservoirs of economic and political power have been systematically withheld from racial and ethnic minorities, causing suffering for many in the human community. People with power have weaponized words to slight, belittle, exclude, and dehumanize. This makes many of us reluctant to claim or use the power available to us. But as we noted, power can be used for different ends—good, bad, and in between. Consider the following example from one of our communities:

In one of the most rapidly growing cities in the United States, real estate developers frequently drive the direction and priorities of political activities. Developers run for city council seats or deputize their associates to pursue them. They use their influence in seats of power to make decisions on behalf of neighborhoods for whom they have no regard or care. Several years ago, a developer wanted to build an area of tall skyscrapers, stadiums, and luxury shopping and housing upstream from the historically Black neighborhoods of the southeastern portion of the city. Already, the Black neighborhoods were built on floodplains because decades prior, that was the only place White leaders would allow them to build. It was clear that this new development would lead to increased flooding that already routinely traumatized Black residents and institutions. Nevertheless, the developer had the power to ignore their concerns and proceed as he desired. That is, until the residents gained power for themselves.

Power, after all, is not just the province of an individual or a business motivated by the maximization of profit and growth. There is also the collective power of people coming together to work to preserve and maintain the dignity of a neighborhood.

Fortunately, the same neighborhood that was poised to become the victim of flooding at the hands of the powerful developer had spent years building their own power. Along with over thirty

Part II. Leading in Community

other houses of worship in the county, the church at the center of the traditionally disempowered Black community had built a great deal of influence through relationships, pooled funds, and organized persistent action. When the development came up for approval at the city council, the neighborhood (with its allies from across the county) demanded an ecological study and for the developer to follow the recommendations of the study to prevent disaster in the neighborhood. Seeing the amount of power this group had, the developer unexpectedly conceded to their demands, something unheard of in the city where this developer held more power than the mayor. Power, in this instance, was responsible for good even though others had intended it for evil, to borrow Joseph's framing in the book of Genesis.[1]

If the church and neighborhood in this example had not consolidated and wielded their influence, their community would have remained at great risk of harm. When we do not use the power available to us to work for the well-being of the community, we are actually abdicating an essential aspect of our leadership role.

> So when they had come together, they asked him, "Lord, is this the time when you will restore the kingdom to Israel?" He replied, "It is not for you to know the times or periods that the Father has set by his own authority. But you will receive power when the Holy Spirit has come upon you; and you will be my witnesses in Jerusalem, in all Judea and Samaria, and to the ends of the earth." When he had said this, as they were watching, he was lifted up, and a cloud took him out of their sight.[2]

We are given the power to give witness to the love of God throughout the world. Our witness comes not only through proclamation but through action. Our words and actions are not inert but are meant to carry within them the power to influence and direct the course of our communities and the lives of our neighbors toward well-being. We follow the example of Jesus, who begins his

---

1. Genesis 50:20.
2. Acts 1:6–9.

ministry by proclaiming economic liberation, the freeing of the incarcerated, and a profound challenge to the political order.[3]

HANDLING POWER

Part of our reticence to wield power as pastors is our recognition that all of us are subject to the temptations of power. We know well the story of the temptation of Christ to claim ultimate authority, salvific power, and invulnerability: "Jesus, full of the Holy Spirit, returned from the Jordan and was led by the Spirit in the wilderness, where for forty days he was tempted by the devil."[4] Jesus resisted the spoils of power, but how are mere humans to do the same? We are especially aware that the church's exercise of power has quite a sordid history, one that often overshadows its positive contributions to scores of people. We also want to avoid slipping into the partisan hypotheticals and ultimatums rife in contemporary society and to avoid being blindsided by our own conceptual limits, experiences, and personal biases. In light of these concerns, how can we ensure that we will be honorable in our use of power? While we are not able to provide an exhaustive treatment here, we want to suggest some helpful ways to begin to think about power, especially to reflect on and learn from work done by pastors in local communities.

FORMS OF POWER

There are two forms of power we'd like you to consider: coercive and noncoercive power. When people think of power, they often think of coercive power first. To challenge the limits of how we think of power, let's begin with power's noncoercive form.

---

3. Luke 4:18–19.
4. Luke 4:1–2a.

PART II. LEADING IN COMMUNITY

Noncoercive Power

Noncoercive power is characterized by a sense of mutuality in the exercise of power. It is a power that makes room for others at the table and uses the art of persuasion rather than force or threat. It has a humble quality and an openness to it. Consider the story of Philip and the Ethiopian eunuch.[5] Both Philip and the eunuch begin their conversation with preconceived notions about the world, but find that their encounter results in both of them being changed. Philip leaves the encounter thinking more broadly about who might be included in the community of faith, and the Ethiopian eunuch leaves with a new imagination about his role in it. Your power can work that way, too.

As a pastor, you have the power to convene members of your congregation and the wider community. You can convene forums in which various stakeholders come together around a crisis or problem in the community. This encounter between members of the community who rarely get in one room and talk with one another can lead to transformation.

A pastor in one of our cohorts grew concerned about the rising level of mistrust of police officers in his community, as well as concern for the very real and particular abuses causing general mistrust. After a headline-grabbing, high-speed chase of a Black teenager that led to a violent arrest, the pastor hosted an event for children in his community. Hundreds came to the event, which was a workshop basically on "how to be arrested safely." Police were present to share their experiences and expectations. But the event was not simply a chance for the police to increase their influence. It also indirectly made the point that some of these policing practices and relationships were not okay. News media came, and the image of a child learning how to hold her hands on the car door outside a rolled-down window in order to lower the level of fear the police had of the occupants of the car spoke volumes. It spurred change without making a direct appeal to civic leaders or trying to wield power to force a change.

---

5. Acts 8:26–40.

Another significant place of the pastor's power is in their preaching. Few leaders have a captive audience as regularly as a pastor. Your preaching can raise awareness of local issues and problems and place them squarely in the context of the Scripture and tradition that governs the Christian life. To preach on social crises is an example of empowering others to think and act by using your power of proclamation. Consider how you can use that power of proclamation in other venues, as well. When asked to give an invocation, open a public meeting, or even simply bless the food at an event, you can introduce values that will help guide your community to address needs in the public square. Proclamation can be persuasive and invitational and elucidate old problems in new ways. In speaking in the public square as a pastor, we are not seeking to coerce others into our viewpoint.

Whether exercising our power to convene the community or proclaim in the public square, we need to do so from a place of humility. We assume the lowest seat in an assembly with the intent of facilitating the assembly's ability to respond to the world around them. We do not take the honored seat at the table but make way for those who have been excluded from the table to sit there. In this way, the pastor as a political leader can catalyze change in the community itself.

Coercive Power

While there is incredible value in noncoercive, persuasive modes of power, sometimes they come up short. To put it perhaps too simply, Jesus must have found persuasion inadequate when the money changers robbed God's children of a "house of prayer for all people" and he turned over the tables.[6] Exclusive use of noncoercive power can sometimes lull you into a state of inaction or apathy where you speak plainly about what *must be done* but the passive voice leads you to stop short of working for any actual change. Sometimes you just need to get it done. In situations where you

---

6. Matthew 21:12–13.

Part II. Leading in Community

employ methods of community organizing or other means of engagement with powerful political leaders, the use of coercive power may be necessary. Coercive power is characterized by the use of force and pressure to effect change that some powerful others resist.

One of us led a broad-based organizing group made up of various religious communities during a local municipal election. One of the candidates up for reelection had sat on the town council for decades and had originally been elected on a platform opposing affordable housing being built near his neighborhood. The politician had a history of skepticism and frequent outright opposition to providing affordable housing in the town. Approached by the community leaders with a proposal for a local affordable housing fund, he rejected the idea outright. When the election came around, however, the councilman came to a candidate forum run by the community organizing group. When he saw the vast array of people present, he reversed course on the spot and endorsed the pastors' plan for establishing a multimillion-dollar housing fund. He relied on this commitment to survive a narrow runoff between himself and another candidate who was adamantly against affordable housing. The politician, in no small way, was coerced by the religious leaders to change his commitments.

This sort of public pressure is instrumental to certain methods of community engagement. Sometimes the self-interest of a person with authority runs counter to your community's interests such that you will find yourself needing to redirect that person's self-interest. In our example, pastors made it the self-interest of the politician to endorse their agenda because of how many voters they had on their side. Did the politician change his mind about housing? We don't know yet. Has his heart changed? We don't know yet. What we do know is that there are now millions of dollars to spend on affordable housing projects in a town that used to be known for opposition to them.

Coercive power frequently goes awry when a desire for domination is at its heart. In the above example, the pastors did not seek to dominate the politician, ask him to switch political parties, or even strip him of his office; rather, they wanted to see him using his power more justly and have it oriented toward the welfare of the city. The pastors could have gathered their communities, declared that the councilman disagreed with their convictions, and worked to beat him in the election. But, that would not have been the work of ministry. Our ministry needs to be relational and focused on transformation, not on forcing the outcome of particular elections. The will to dominate cannot be at the center of our work with power.

In the story of the pastors working to stymie the public leader opposed to affordable housing, it might have been a temptation for the pastors to cast the issue as "we are good and he is evil because we care about people and he only cares about profits." Such framings let the camel's nose of coercion under the tent of power. The public official had a different vision of "the good" from the pastors' vision. He thought that the economic benefits of having fewer housing options but at a higher price point outweighed the good of having more housing at affordable levels. There is thus a "grace of self-doubt" in healthy, noncoercive leaders that resists temptations to vilify. The ancient rhetorical practice of *dissoi logoi* is instructive here: before responding to your opponent, you should put their view into different words than the ones they used, but still such that they would say of your rephrasing, "Yes, that's my view." Only then is the opposing view offered. These kinds of moments are pauses that honor eschatology; we see in a mirror dimly[7] and wait for the end to see how much our discernment got right and how and when we were wrong.

POWER AND LOVE

Rightly directing your power so it is not simply domination requires attention to the beating heart behind your use of power. This is at the core of the pastor's reflection on their role as a political leader. What animates your ministry? What directs you toward

---

7. 1 Corinthians 13:12.

Part II. Leading in Community

these issues? Is it wrath, mere passion, or casual interest? None of those will sustain your work. Instead, when considering your power, you must consider love.

It is also invaluable to share openly and with vulnerability to your clergy community about your struggles with and displays of power. Ask for accountability and to be held to a theological grounding. A diverse group of peers who represent a different relationship to power in your community is life-giving and will provide holy responses. If you're bulldozing or strong-arming, they'll tell you. You will find the deep roots of connections to all humanity if this work is voiced.

Oscar Romero said this about power while working under far more dangerous and demanding conditions: "Power is good, but abuse by humans has made it something to fear. All has been created by God, but humans have subjected it to sin."[8] The same power that forges a sword can forge a sickle: what matters is the purpose and spirit behind the use of power. The spirit behind the sword is domination and the spirit of the sickle is harvest and provision. Yet both require power.

Much as Paul reminds us in the classic passage from 1 Corinthians 13, all the community work you do will be useless without the centrality of love. If you do not love your neighbor, it's unlikely you're going to work for their welfare. If you do not love your community, it's unlikely you will be invested in its betterment for the long haul. Your exercises of power will eventually degenerate into forms of domination or mere self-service without love at the center.

The story goes that Martin Luther King Jr. was asked to write down what he believed was the meaning of love. There exists a small note card bearing his signature with the statement, "Love is the greatest force in the universe. It is the heartbeat of the moral cosmos. He who loves is a participant in the being of God."[9] If you want any of your community engagement to be distinct from simple political activism or secular organizing work and if you want it

---

8. Romero, *Violence of Love*, 60.
9. Lee, "Rare Handwritten Note."

to participate in the holy work you and your church are called to, it must have love at the center. In that way, it participates in the life of God. "God is love, and those who abide in love abide in God, and God abides in them."[10]

---

10. 1 John 4:16b.

PART III

Persisting in Community

8

Expecting and Managing Resistance

TENSION AS OPPORTUNITY FOR CHANGE

Tension, as in every organizational system, is a normal facet of congregational life. Many pastors are familiar with the frustration of wanting to lead change in the church, whether as simple as forming a new ministry or as controversial as replacing the carpet in the sanctuary. Pastors can face resistance from a small group of detractors or even the majority of the congregation. The prospect of change always produces tension. In and of itself, tension is neither positive nor negative; it is a neutral entity that can swing back and forth on an organizational pendulum. Too much tension in a system can lead to conflict and cut off relationships; too little tension can lead to stagnation and reinforce the status quo.

How a pastor manages these tensions usually determines the outcome. In our experience, pastors are usually catalysts for change in the church, but the congregation often prefers the comfort of the status quo. Raise your hand if you've ever encountered the old congregational proverb, "But we've never done it that way before?" This phrase is, indeed, the bane of many pastors' existence.

Part III. Persisting in Community

There are many reasons why churches resist change, especially when it comes to engaging the broader community. Some view themselves as an anointed clique, and they don't want to contaminate their holiness by looking out the windows. Others may not have any windows—or they may be physically isolated or demographically segregated from their community. Or they may simply lack the imagination to see where or how they might make a difference in their city or town.

Another reason why some churches resist their pastors embracing the role of a political leader is that it conflicts with their idea of pastoral leadership. Many churches view their pastors as hired hands who only tend to the acute needs of the flock. Or they may compare the church to a country club, where the pastor organizes the activities and keeps the building in shape. They may see the church simply as a "hospice house" where the pastor's primary responsibility is to hold the hand of the sick and bury the dead. Unfortunately, some churches just lack vision for the public square and are, therefore, reluctant to accept their pastor as a political leader.

On the other hand, we have to admit that sometimes the congregation wants change and desires a more robust role in the community, but the pastor is the one who is entrenched in homeostasis. Have you ever heard the phrase, "You can't teach an old dog new tricks"? Some pastors lack the imagination to do anything more than sit in their cushy studies, read their theological books, write sixteen-page sermons, and conduct an occasional wedding or funeral. They hardly have the capacity to empathize with family dysfunctions and emotional problems in their congregation, let alone have the ambition to meet with a mayor to mobilize relief efforts after a tornado or flood.

That being said, the vast majority of pastors in our cohorts have expressed deep frustration due to their congregations' resistance toward their efforts to lead change.[1] This may be especially

---

1. As a collective group of authors from different denominational traditions, we, again, debated the use of a word. This time, we did not agree on the perception of resistance and whether the congregation was most often the resistor. Our various denominational polities lend themselves to more or less reliance on the pastor as leader or the congregation as leader. Thus, the

true when it comes to the pastor embracing the role of a political leader and motivating the church to be more active in the community. But tension, if managed well, can be a place of opportunity for leading effective change in the church and transformation in the community.

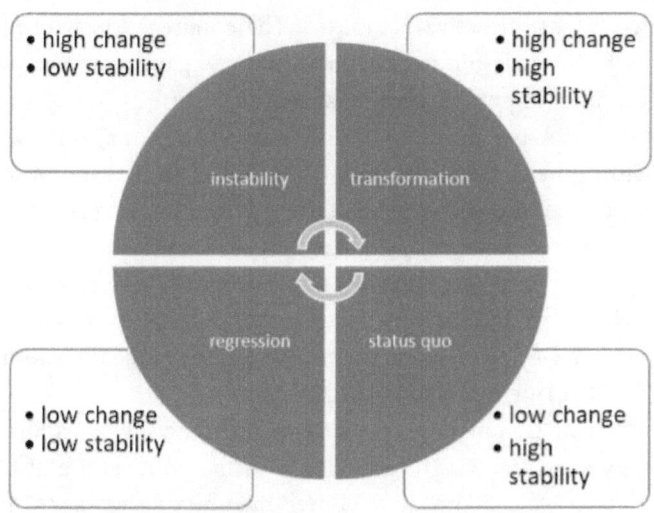

In an environment of low tension and high stability, the lack of tension leads to the maintenance of a status quo—just or not. Unless the pastor or the congregation injects tension into the system, nothing will ever change and the church will slowly enter a coma or inactivity or eventually die. Similarly, low tension and low stability can lead to regression. Change occurs, but it is backsliding into old patterns and habits in the absence of leadership, which can produce undesirable results like bigotry or exclusion grounded in fear. When there is high tension in the presence of low stability, chaos results, and not much good is possible. When tension is high and stability is high, however, there's a true possibility of change and transformation. Existing in that space, however, requires a grounded and committed leader like the ones we've been describing in this book.

---

different approaches to this symbiotic relationship may produce greater or lesser resistance to change.

Part III. Persisting in Community

Tensions can arise from many places and take on many forms within the life of the church. The congregation may be unable to see beyond the partisanship of conservative and liberal cable news talking points, for example. Because these harsh viewpoints shape our public discourse, it may be difficult for pastors and parishioners to see issues from the same perspective. This discontent produces tension between the two. The congregation may resist the pastor's leadership toward community engagement because it fears conflict or prefers safety and security.

Occasionally, the church is resistant to but not against working within the community. Rather, there is resistance to the spiritual direction, the gospel presentation, or the sovereignty of God. These congregations enjoy their role as saviors, social workers, or therapists; plumbers, carpenters, or painters; gift-givers, beneficiaries, or funders so much that they have no desire to be seen as a conduit for God's grace, mercy, and love. They value the spotlight and the accolades and lack humility.

One of us ran into this sort of resistance when adjusting their role and the congregation's role in the political life of their community. A small group of church members grew weary of the noncoercive power exercised in the pulpit week after week. The pastor encouraged the membership through prayers and sermons toward local issues—including issues facing other church members in their daily lives! Because these issues did not concern this particular group, they circulated a petition to ask the pastors to direct attention almost exclusively to visits and pastoral care while focusing on sermons that would make church members feel good and leave the sanctuary happy every Sunday. As this effort emerged during the COVID-19 pandemic, there was little opportunity for direct confrontation to stop the small group's would-be mutiny. The group engaged in a coordinated campaign of harassment against the ministers and leadership of the church. At the root of the resistance was a marked distaste for the political role their ministers and the wider church had assumed, which only after a long conflict were they able to honestly articulate. The splinter group and the rest of the church were at an irreconcilable impasse.

Expecting and Managing Resistance

What can a pastor do to respond to a congregation that resists their political leadership? Of course, we trust that you have done the work previously mentioned in this book. However, we also know that some congregations just feel immovable. This is when it is time to ask if this resistance is representative of the whole or a part. Is it just the loudest voices, the most established members, the greatest donors, or the meanest individuals who are showing defiance? Be careful not to allow their clout to overshadow the majority. Ask if they are a splinter or a cancer. A splinter can be removed from the body—it may be painful, and if deep enough, it may require cutting something (or really someone) away. But the body will heal and move on eventually. However, if it is cancer, it requires so much triage and treatment to eliminate what is harmful to the body that the church and the pastor may not be able to move forward together.

USING TENSION, RESOLVING CONFLICT

Managing tension and overcoming resistance takes the careful use of pastoral capital. This term describes the credibility that a pastor earns over time. Credibility is gained by cultivating loving relationships and exhibiting competent leadership, and it often involves taking calculated risks, maintaining a non-anxious presence in times of tension, and admitting mistakes when you're wrong. Long-tenured pastors usually have more capital than new pastors, and the pastor's level of emotional maturity is another critical factor. But once pastors stockpile some pastoral capital, they have to make difficult decisions about where and when to cash in. In our experience, resistance to change is often the right place to spend it.

Pastors have a plethora of tools at their disposal for managing tension in the church. You can use sermons, personal conversations, Bible studies, videos, newsletter articles, and stories to introduce tension into the system to help churches take on a more active role in the community. You can also tone down the tension and calm the congregation's fears by promising and practicing clear communication, consensus building, trial periods,

Part III. Persisting in Community

and an incremental pace for change. When they engage with their community, together the church and the community can embrace beauty, art, and creativity; they flow with love, healing, and wholeness; they welcome messiness, forgiveness, and transformation; they have a sense of belonging, inclusion, and reconciliation; and they feel the overwhelming joy of new life. The church will more fully embody Christ's teaching of hospitality by receiving all to the table.

From the point of view of the pastor, a congregation uninterested in seeking to advance its mission by joining its efforts with those of community partners can start to seem like an unsettling problem. From the point of view of the congregation, the situation seems a bit different. Most congregants are members of congregations that they like and value. It worries them to see their pastor spending more and more time engaging in community concerns. They might wonder if the pastor cares about them anymore. But the pastor who has been gaining experience learning about and working in, for example, healthcare, might well be a better congregational pastor as a result of that information. She might be able to give better advice to the adult daughter of an aging parent who is struggling to understand how to think about quality at the end of life for her loved one. A pastor who has real relationships with workers in the criminal justice system may be a far more effective pastoral counselor for the parents of a child who has been arrested or was the victim of a crime. Proximity to and knowledge about the beating heart of a local community is not a distraction for a parish pastor. They are forms of excellence and faithfulness in parish ministry.

We would be remiss if we did not mention that sometimes the wider community is resistant to the congregation. One of our programs from the Midwest embarked on a study tour in the Pacific Northwest. Religious institutions and leaders in the Midwest tend to be trusted, or at least tolerated, far more than in the latter. Many would-be political leader pastors spoke of the difficulty of speaking publicly or even convening semi-publicly on a social issue if they represented even a perceived religious perspective. One local church hosted a lecture series on poverty and the attendees were shocked and kind of upset that the famous theological speaker mentioned Jesus a lot during his talk. There may be less need for community mobilization in these kinds of secularized contexts because residents unaffiliated with a religious tradition are often more politically active in part to compensate for the vacuum that religion has otherwise historically filled. But there are special challenges in doing community-based ministry in contexts where the sign at an event sponsored by a church needs to have the church's name in a tiny font at the bottom of the banner if they want people to come.

THE EMPATHY BELOW THE TENSION

One of our directors was hosting a new cohort of fourteen pastors at their first gathering in the mountains of North Carolina. After three rich days of telling their personal stories, discussing adaptive leadership, and naming their hopes and dreams for their time in the program, they gathered for a final theological reflection conversation. The crisp September air whispered across their faces as they listened to the birds call to one another. A doe and fawn paraded across the lawn. They were less skeptical of one another, but they were still not companions. They knew facts about each person: some lived in rural communities, some in big and small cities, some in tourist towns on the coast, and some in the suburbs. Almost equal in gender identity, they were very diverse in denominational identity, age, race, and socioeconomic status, as well as their respective ministry roles. And yet, here they were together, committed to sharing their experiences of ministry, and covenanted to share honesty and integrity. All were excited about the common purpose to see the transformative power that comes from intentionally engaging the multiple layers of community around them.

The director began the session by reading an article about compassion fatigue.

Part III. Persisting in Community

> Compassion fatigue is a state of mind in which we become less and less able to help others, for fear of being hurt ourselves. We're talking about natural processes—namely, compassion, and empathy—being put to use over and over again in highly repetitive, artificial situations. That kind of work will wear down even the strongest person...The symptoms and consequences of compassion fatigue include: depression, anxiety, hypochondria, combativeness, the sensation of being on fast-forward, and an inability to concentrate.[2]

Immediately the participants' body language indicated that they connected to this feeling. After three years of leading a congregation through COVID-19, the external exhaustion of American politics, more funerals and hospital visits than ever before, and on and on, they were exhausted. But it was not just the weight of the times—everyone in a caring profession was feeling this burden. It was the added layer that they were carrying a congregation on their shoulders. And now they have enrolled in a program to embrace the possibly divisive role of political leader. They were going to be challenged to deeply learn about their communities, respond to greater and more significant issues, and address power. It almost seemed too much to bear.

The director allowed them time to process and grieve. Almost every minister shared a story about the current resistance of their congregation and their fear of what may happen next as they embarked on this next phase of leadership because of the program. The director was soaked in the tangible pain that was hovering over the group like fog.

"You are Jesus in Gethsemane; for years, stuck in the Garden. You can barely stand. You do not want to face what is to come, even though you know you must be faithful to follow the journey wherever it leads next. You feel alone, drained, depleted. And you turn to your congregants, as Jesus did to his disciples. 'All I need from you is to STAY AWAKE! Pray with me!' And even still, asleep

---

2. Smith, "What Happens When Compassion Hurts."

Expecting and Managing Resistance

they were. The same is your congregation, unable to do the very minimum to hold you together."

The generative response that came from this encounter together is important to identify. First, it was as simple as the naming of their collective pain, tension, and fear. And then the recognition that the other clergy in the group understood to a bone-deep level. No matter how healthy a congregation may be, they cannot hold you together the way your colleagues in ministry can. A fellow minister can pray with and for you and lighten your load. Even though this magical moment did not change any minister's situation, it gave them renewed resiliency for what they faced in the months between their gatherings.

Ultimately, we're inviting pastors to expand their vocational horizons to the public square. This is not for the sake of itself but because we believe it is a central concern of pastoral ministry. Political leadership may also be just what you need to reinvigorate a stagnant career or summon the courage to start one. This work is worth it, and it comes with a deep sense of satisfaction and fulfillment that sustains pastors for the long haul. And when you can do this in a community with other clergy, the challenges somehow seem like they can be overcome.

9

The Joy of Ministry in Community

WE HOPE OUR VISION for life together—where you participate in a diverse learning community with other clergy, grow into a new perspective of the pastor as a political leader, and mobilize your church to meet the surrounding needs—will result in the transformative power we have seen that emerges when clergy engage the multiple layers of community around them.

One of the co-authors remembers when their pastoral learning cohort first gathered. Initially, they knew nothing of one another besides what they chose to share in their submitted biographies. As the months and years progressed, they ate, traveled, debated, read, and learned together, and caught increasingly intimate glimpses into each other's lives and ministries. They learned the lower half of each other's faces when the masks came off following COVID-19 restrictions. Children of the pastors made appearances when their spouses came to claim them at the end of a cohort retreat. They wrestled with emerging vaccines, end-of-life planning, racism in educational opportunities and bus systems, and the absence of artistic beauty in late-modern Christian life. They stayed up late like they were back in college and almost lost a few of their members on overseas flight complications while they traveled together. And from that space of shared vocation, curiosity, learning, and adventure, they formed a community that was increasingly honest and tender. They prayed for each other when they were sick and supported each other when their churches went through difficult times. One of their members lost a baby, and they grieved with him in the line for coffee in downtown Boston when he was reaching for his wallet and instead pulled something out of his pocket which reminded him of his loss. They found community on the way.

There is a novel by Wendell Berry titled *Jayber Crow*. Like many of Berry's books, this one extols the virtues of staying put in a place and committing to a community. Unlike his other books, this one is about a barber. But in some interesting ways, a barber in a small Kentucky town has a lot in common with the vision of ministry this book has been holding up. Everyone in the town knows the barber. The number of topics of conversation about the community from and around the barber's chair is astronomical. Jayber, the barber, is the master of his own calendar, and he sets his own priorities. He is connected to so many tendrils in his community. He is a nodal point of relationships and a storehouse of information and histories—real and imagined—about his people.

He is also an unmarried man who suffers in the name of beauty. The barber's initials, J. C., may indicate what Berry had in mind when creating Jayber Crow. His apartment is the upper level of his shop, a bit like a parsonage of old. If no one is in the barber's chair during good weather, Jayber tends his rows in the garden out back and returns when the bell on the shop door bids him. He may hear that widow Elkins needs a delivery of groceries, so he drives down Red Oak Road and brings her some. She's grateful and gives him too many eggs, which he sets on the table by his door for someone hungry to take. Jayber had been an orphan, raised briefly by extended family but then plucked up and removed to an orphanage. He has been in what has become his community for decades, with only a recent absence for a short stint in seminary before he dropped that idea and returned.

Jayber reflects on the shock of being pulled out of his community and sent to the orphanage, only to return and begin to feel at home.

Part III. Persisting in Community

> But when I recognized Burley Coulter on the water that morning and told him who I was, and he remembered me from that lost and gone and given-up old time and then introduced me to people as the boy Aunt Cordie and Uncle Othy took to raise—well, that changed me. After all those years of keeping myself aloof and alone, I began to feel tugs from the outside. I felt my life branching and forking out into the known world. In a way, I was almost sorry. It was as though I knew without exactly knowing, or feeling, or smelling in the air, the already accomplished fact that nothing would ever be simple for me again. I never again would be able to put my life in a box and carry it away.[1]

Pastors are often asked to put their lives into a box and carry it away. It is one of the few professions left with expectations of moving multiple times, sometimes by great distances. And pastors rarely minister in the community of their origin, perhaps because, as Jesus said, "Prophets are not without honor, except in their hometown, and among their own kin, and in their own house."[2] But even so many people do not ever achieve the kind of connectedness with a community a pastor can. This is, in some senses, an obligation of the pastor, whose job it is to visit, listen, support people, and be a public presence. But, more than an obligation, it can become a gift, an utter joy.

When Jayber drives down the road to bring the widow her groceries, it is a fundamentally different act than an Amazon driver doing the "same" thing. He sees the world differently from someone just passing through. While a transitory observer may see the superficial connections between people, Jayber sees his community on a deeper level. He perceives an invisible web, a network of mutuality, that goes beyond the relationship between a customer and a cashier, a teacher and a student, a doctor and a patient. The pastor, like Jayber, needs to see how the doctor relates to that cashier when they sit on the same pew at church, how the student and the customer are adversarial neighbors, and how the

---

1. Berry, *Jayber Crow* 130.
2. Mark 6:4.

teacher and the patient are one and the same. The pastor is in a unique situation to see us for more than the simple relationships we have with each other. If we're attentive enough to the connections that we've described in this book, like Jayber we'll begin to feel as if this "invisible web . . .was as real as the ground it was woven over."[3] Rooted like a tall tree, pastors can see so much more if they lean into the opportunity to do so.

Even when a policy change is implemented well, even when the correct funds are raised, and even when procedures of good governance are followed—the church and its pastors know that there is always something more. Something critical remains undone. Our hope and even our expectation is for everyone to "have life and have it abundantly."[4] That hope, though, ultimately lies in what is beyond us—our hope is in God. This is the difference that it makes to have pastors involved in community issues. Our clergy leadership programs have, for instance, examined criminal justice and the reforms needed to address systemic racism and ineffective and wasteful practices. Let's say we implement all the reforms we want to see. Even so, they are not justice. The tears of the friends and family of a murder victim are not wiped away, never to return, simply because of rational policy and wise implementation. There's still the need for something more.

A member of one of our cohorts grew ever more passionate about community engagement as a result of learning more about their state and local context. In fact, he was so eager to commit more fully to this work that he left parish ministry. He worked in a local nonprofit advocacy office. Then he moved to a state-level lobbyist position. Eventually, he realized the persistence of a certain emptiness inside, even when doing the work he loved (and was very good at). The emptiness was a congregation-sized hole. So, he returned to the parish and found ways of engaging and improving his community while wearing a clerical collar instead of a necktie. Now, he celebrates communion with students and townspeople whose hopes and struggles he knows because of being in

3. Berry, *Jayber Crow*, 131.
4. John 10:10.

Part III. Persisting in Community

community with them. This experience drives him to engage in making their city just a little bit better. The dialectic of moving from leadership to community and back again has sustained him in his ministry. It has supplied him with friendships too numerous to count. It has revealed the invisible web of meaning and connection in his community that practically sings out as he makes his way through it. If that's not joy in ministry, it's pretty close.

Just think of all you have to offer and all you have to receive as a pastor. As a political leader, you're a reservoir of the hopes and dreams, agonies and grief, connections and ruptures within not just your congregation but in the whole community. You become a nexus God can use for the healing and transformation of not just yourself but your congregation, your neighborhood, and your city. After all, we carry in our bodies, relationships, and actions the God "who by the power at work within us is able to accomplish abundantly far more than all we can ask or imagine."[5] God invites us into a shared life that promises transformation for everyone.

Our community work, more than the practical tools we've given you, is an extension of God's grace to the world. Into the complexities, messiness, and struggles of our own "invisible web," we bring the peace and justice of the God who cares deeply for all of our pain and longing. What you have to offer your community, and receive from it, is more than a policy change. It is the revolutionary beauty of a renewed life together.

---

5. Ephesians 3:20.

Bibliography

Ashford, Bruce Riley. *Every Square Inch: An Introduction to Cultural Engagement for Christians*. Bellingham, WA: Lexham, 2014.
Augustine, Jonathan C. *When Prophets Preach*. Minneapolis: Fortress, 2023.
Berry, Wendell. *Jayber Crow*. Washington, DC: Counterpoint, 2000.
Bolsinger, Tod E. *Canoeing the Mountains: Christian Leadership in Uncharted Territory*. Downers Grove, IL: InterVarsity, 2018.
Bonhoeffer, Dietrich. *Life Together*. Dietrich Bonhoeffer Works, vol. 5. Translated by James Burtness et al. Minneapolis: Fortress, 1996.
Brooks, Jonathan. *Church Forsaken: Practicing Presence in Neglected Neighborhoods*. Downers Grove, IL: InterVarsity, 2018.
Busch, Eberhard. *Karl Barth: His Life from Letters and Autobiographical Texts*. Translated by John Bowden. Philadelphia: Fortress, 1976.
Chambers, Edward. *Roots for Radicals: Organizing for Power, Action, and Justice*. London: Bloomsbury, 2018.
Conder, Tim, and Daniel Rhodes. *Organizing Church*. St. Louis: Chalice, 2017.
Cone, James. *Black Theology and Black Power*. Maryknoll, NY: Orbis, 1968.
Cooke, William. *Canary in the Coal Mine*. Carol Stream, IL: Tyndale Momentum, 2021.
Creech, R. Robert. *Family Systems and Congregational Life: A Map for Ministry*. Grand Rapids: Baker Academic, 2019.
Fernandez, Linda. "Empathy and Social Justice: The Power of Proximity in Improvement Science." Carnegie Foundation for the Advancement of Teaching, April 21, 2016. https://www.carnegiefoundation.org/blog/empathy-and-social-justice-the-power-of-proximity-in-improvement-science/.
Friedman, Edwin H. *Generation to Generation: Family Process in Church and Synagogue*. New York: Guilford, 2011.
Friesen, Dwight, Tim Soerens, and Paul Sparks. *The New Parish: How Neighborhood Churches Are Transforming Mission, Discipleship, and Community*. Downers Grove, IL: InterVarsity, 2014.
Fromm, Erich, and Rainer Funk. *The Art of Listening*. New York: Open Road Integrated Media, 2013.

BIBLIOGRAPHY

Frost, Michael. *Surprise the World: Five Habits of Highly Missional People.* Colorado Springs: NavPress, 2016.

Frost, Michael, and Alan Hirsch. *The Shaping of Things to Come: Innovation and Mission for the 21st-Century Church.* Grand Rapids: Baker, 2013.

Greenwood Forest Baptist Church. *Inhospitable: A Deportation Story* (2019). inhospitableusa.org.

Heifetz, Ronald A., Alexander Grashow, and Martin Linsky. *The Practice of Adaptive Leadership: Tools and Tactics for Changing Your Organization and the World.* Boston: Harvard Business Press, 2009.

Heifetz, Ronald, and Marty Linsky. *Leadership on the Line.* Boston: Harvard Business Review Press, 2017.

Heltzel, Peter, and Alexia Salvatierra. *Faith-Rooted Organizing: Mobilizing Church in Service to the World.* Downers Grove, IL: Intervarsity, 2013.

Herrington, Jim, Trisha Taylor, and R. Robert Creech. *The Leader's Journey: Accepting the Call to Personal and Congregational Transformation.* Grand Rapids: Baker Academic, 2020.

Horn, David, and Jason R. McConnell. *Return to the Parish: The Pastor in the Public Square.* Eugene, OR: Cascade, 2022.

Horowitz, Rosemary. *Elie Wiesel and the Art of Storytelling.* Jefferson, NC: McFarland, 2014.

Hummel, Charles E. *The Tyranny of the Urgent.* Downers Grove, IL: InterVarsity, 1994.

Hunter, James Davison. *To Change the World: The Irony, Tragedy, and Possibility of Christianity in the Late Modern World.* New York: Oxford University Press, 2010.

Kidder, Tracy. *Rough Sleepers.* New York: Random House, 2023.

King, Martin Luther, Jr. "Letter from a Birmingham Jail." In *Why We Can't Wait*, 64–84. London: Penguin, 1964.

King, Patrick. *How to Listen, Hear, and Validate.* Self-published, 2021.

Lamott, Anne. *Bird by Bird: Instructions on Writing and Life.* New York: Anchor, 1995.

Lee, Alicia. "Martin Luther King Jr. Explains the Meaning of Love in Rare Handwritten Note." *CNN*, February 9, 2020. https://www.cnn.com/2020/02/09/us/martin-luther-king-jr-handwritten-note-for-sale-trnd/index.html.

Lee, Jak Joon. *The Great World House: Martin Luther King, Jr. and Global Ethics.* Cleveland, OH: Pilgrim, 2011.

Lupton, Robert D. *Toxic Charity: How Churches and Charities Hurt Those They Help, and How to Reverse It.* San Francisco: HarperOne, 2012.

The Mayor's Task Force on Institutional Racism and Systemic Inequalities. "Final Report (2017)." https://cityofaustin.github.io/institutional-racism/.

National Council on Family Relations. "Inclusion and Diversity Committee Report: What's Your Social Location?" April 4, 2019. https://www.ncfr.org/ncfr-report/spring-2019/inclusion-and-diversity-social-location.

Nelson, Derek R. "Pastors Have the Power to Convene Conversation." *Christian Century*, September 27, 2017, 12–14.

Niebuhr, Reinhold. *Reinhold Niebuhr: Major Works on Religion and Politics*. Washington, DC: Library of Congress, 2015.

Nouwen, Henri J. M. *The Wounded Healer: Ministry in Contemporary Society*. London: Darton, Longman & Todd, 2014.

O'Malley, Ed, and Amanda Cebula. *Your Leadership Edge*. Portland, OR: Bard, 2022.

Peterson, Eugene H. *Working the Angles: The Shape of Pastoral Integrity*. Grand Rapids: Eerdmans, 1987.

Placher, William C., and Derek R. Nelson. *Readings in the History of Christian Theology*. Volume 2. Louisville: Westminster John Knox, 2015.

Rogers, Melissa. *Faith in American Public Life*. Waco, TX: Baylor University Press, 2019.

Romero, Oscar Arnulfo. *The Violence of Love*. Austin: University of Texas Press, 1998.

Scazzero, Peter. *The Emotionally Healthy Leader: How Transforming Your Inner Life Will Deeply Transform Your Church, Team, and the World*. Grand Rapids: Zondervan, 2015.

Smith, Jeremy. "What Happens When Compassion Hurts." *Greater Good Magazine*, https://greatergood.berkeley.edu/article/item/what_happens_when_compassion_hurts.

Steinke, Peter L. *How Your Twenty-First-Century Church Family Works: Understanding Congregations as Emotional Systems*. Lanham, MD: Rowman & Littlefield, 2021.

This Cultural Moment Podcast, by Bridgetown Church in Portland, Oregon, USA and Red Church, Melbourne, Australia.

Thurman, Howard. *Jesus and the Disinherited*. Boston: Beacon, 1996.

Tolkien, J. R. R. *The Two Towers*. New York: HarperCollins, 2014.

Vengoechea, Ximena. *Listen Like You Mean It: Reclaiming the Lost Art of True Connection*. New York: Penguin, 2021.

"Why Do a Book Sprint?" Book Sprints, https://guidelines.booksprints.net/docs/0_description/.

Will, Barbara. *Prophetic Leadership and Visionary Hope*. Philadelphia: University of Pennsylvania Press, 2023.

Wilson-Hartgrove, Jonathan. *Revolution of Values: Reclaiming Public Faith for the Common Good*. Downers Grove, IL: InterVarsity, 2019.

Wink, Walter. *The Powers That Be: Theology for a New Millennium*. New York: Doubleday, 1998.

www.ingramcontent.com/pod-product-compliance
Lightning Source LLC
Chambersburg PA
CBHW020933180426
43192CB00036B/934